Costa Brava

GW01459512

Roger Büdeler

Costa Brava

Catalonia East – Pyrenees to Barcelona

Translated by Tom Krupp

50 selected valley and mountain walks

With 78 colour photographs,
50 walking maps with a scale of 1:25,000 / 1:50,000 / 1:75,000
and an overview map with a scale of 1:650,000

ROTHER · MUNICH

Cover photograph:
Cap de Creus

Frontispiece (page 2):
Montserrat: View of the Agulles

All photographs are by the author.

Cartography:
Walking maps with a scale of 1:25,000 / 1:50,000 / 1:75,000
Rolle-Kartografie, Holzkirchen
Overview maps with a scale of 1:650,000 and 1:1,200,000
© Freytag & Berndt, Vienna

1st edition 2006

© Bergverlag Rother GmbH, Munich

ISBN 3-7633-4833-6
ISBN 13: 978-3-7633-4833-6

Preface

Spain's »wild coast« is still one of the most popular holiday spots in the Iberian Peninsula. In contrast to the other well-known, excessively-developed tourist regions, the Costa Brava remains relatively untouched. Naturally, hotel high-rises, fenced-in beaches and spaghetti junctions have appeared here as well, but among them, many stretches of pristine natural landscape have survived and the truly untamed aspects of the coastline have endured: miles of coastal cliffs, bizarrely formed mountains, and solitary beaches and bays with crystal-clear water. The northern Cap de Creus between Llança and Roses sets a pattern for the wide variety of landscapes that merge together on the Costa Brava. Walks along the »wild coast« need not necessarily be restricted to the lovely and exciting trails found on the coastlines between Portbou and Lloret de Mar – directly on the rugged seaboard, along coastal cliffs high above the sea or descending to sheltered bays. One should not forget the backdrop of the Costa Brava – the mountainous interior where densely wooded mountain ridges climb to sub-alpine heights, where sheer-faced high plateaux sprawl or where surreal rock formations tower above their flat surroundings. In other areas, verdant volcanic domes nestle near pre-Pyrenean peaks and jagged »islands« of granite loom out of expansive lowlands. All of this is only a stone's throw from the seashore and within easy reach of the seaside resorts and coastal beaches. Scenic variety can hardly be more tempting, especially when many of the walking regions are also protected natural parks.

From the coast to the mountains, from sea to crag, from sandy beach to shady Mediterranean forest – the diverse and changing natural landscapes exert a powerful attraction for walkers on the Costa Brava. Naturally, you can choose the other way around: starting from the pretty spots in the countryside to take a walking tour towards the sea. The »joy of discovery« knows no limits and a wide spectrum of walking routes offers numerous opportunities to satisfy every fancy and demand: from the leisurely »camí de ronda« on the border between land and sea through to challenging summit tours, from an ecological nature trail traversing a unique marshland through to a rocky route incorporating some enjoyable scrambling. With a few exceptions, the suggested routes are easy to moderately difficult and are scheduled in time frames of half a day so that ample opportunity is given for additional exploration of the natural landscapes, scenery and culture of this area.

I wish you many enjoyable and eventful days of walking on Spain's »wild coast«!

Spring 2006   Roger Büdeler

Contents

Tourist Information

Use of the Guide

An overview map preceding the description of the walking region pinpoints the location of the individual walks. Before the route description, the most important information needed to plan and carry out the individual walk is at first summarized under a list of key points. A short depiction of the route is meant to provide a general impression; this is followed by the actual walk description from starting point to destination and – for a circular walk – back to the starting point. Coloured mini-maps for the individual walks show the course of the route but are not very precise so we recommend carrying an additional topographical map. The Index lists all walking destinations, place names, starting and finishing points and all important points en route. A little language guide for the relevant Catalonian terms concerning the walks can be found at the very end of the book.

Grade

Of course, walks on the Costa Brava and in the mountainous interior cannot be compared with Alpine tours. Also the degree of difficulty and exertion awaiting the walker varies according to the individual route. Certain requirements are demanded to ensure the safety of the walker and to make sure that the experience is always enjoyable. Mediterranean ambience and relatively low elevations rarely exceeding 1700m should not lead to carelessness. Some walks require physical fitness, sure-footedness, a good sense of direction and a good head for heights. The difficulty of the routes is differentiated by the colouring of the walk numbers; specific demands are listed in the key points for the individual tour. Grades are indicated as follows:

Even particular walkers get their money's worth.

BLUE

These are safe and easy walks along trails and paths that are usually clearly marked. The length of time needed for the tour is limited. Ascents are usually moderate. Short but strenuous stretches may still be included. Extreme differences in height are spread out over longer distances.

RED

These are moderately difficult walks requiring a certain degree of walking experience. Differences in height, tour lengths and ascent demand more strength, stamina and walking skills. Some stretches of trail lead over precipitous terrain and require an excellent head for heights. An indistinct or poorly-marked route demands a good sense of direction as well.

BLACK

These are difficult walks with great differences in height, longer walking times and steep stretches. These routes require not only good physical fitness and plenty of stamina but also a great degree of sure-footedness in troublesome terrain and may include some stretches of scrambling.

Dangers

As a rule, the routes follow well-established trails, both forestry trails and old local paths. In the mountainous regions, expect climatic quirks especially when reaching highland elevations. Despite being close to the Mediterranean, snow cover can be found for longer periods in winter; in springtime expect sudden temperature drops and snowfall. The north-eastern region of the Costa Brava in particular is plagued by the tramuntana, a stormy north wind that makes walking along the cliff coast and along precipitous trails very dangerous. The coolness of the tramuntana in unsheltered terrain can make a walk extremely exhausting. Depending on the season, the sun's rays create yet another risk which should not be taken lightly, especially in the cooler mountains or along the windy coast. Sufficient drinks should be carried along and an effective protection from the sun (sunscreen/hat/sunglasses) are essential.

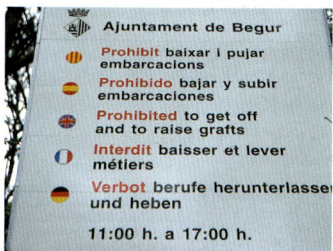

Lost in Translation? Actually launching boats here is not permitted.

Equipment

Sturdy walking shoes – or even mountain climbing boots – and practical clothing for protection from rain and cold are required. Trekking poles are extremely useful in difficult and/or steep terrain. A little emergency medical kit should be packed away in a knapsack during any walk. Since most of the walks lack opportunities for refreshment along the way, be sure to carry enough food and drink. A detailed walking map drawn to a small scale should also form part of your standard kit.

Walking times

Not precise to the minute! Since the actual time needed for a walk naturally depends on the individual's stride and fitness as well as on unforeseen hindrances along the route, the cited walking times represent only an average rate. They are based on mean walking speed and do not take rest breaks or other interruptions into consideration.

Getting there

Unfortunately only a few walks can be approached by public transportation without facing a great deal of complication. Because of the limited number of bus connections and scheduled services, the walker is largely dependent on a private vehicle. When it is necessary to drive on a forestry track to reach the starting point, this will be indicated in the individual tour description.

Best times of the year

It is best to avoid the summer heat – that means the sweltering months of July and August! Routes in the high mountains are exceptions to the rule. Naturally the decisive factor is the current weather situation; even in the summer one can expect cool winds on the coast and in the mountainous interior. Other than that, the Costa Brava is ideal walking country all year round, with unique seasonal charms: an unexpected riot of flowers in early summer, colourful woodland landscapes in autumn and a fantastic light in winter.

Maps

The mini walking maps of the tour descriptions provide orientation for the course of the walk. In addition, we recommend maps drawn to a smaller scale. The material available in Spain is for the most part sound and up-to-date. Most walking maps can also be ordered in your own country. Locally, you can procure them in bookshops, kiosks and tourist information offices. Bookshops specializing in a wide assortment of travel publications can be found in Barcelona and Girona, both offering sales over the internet. Llibreria Altaïr, Gran Vía 616, 08007 Barcelona; www.altair.es and Llibreria Ulyssus, Calle Ballesteries 29, 17004 Girona; www.ulyssus.com.

Nature and environmental protection

Aside from the general rules of conduct concerning environmental protection, natural parks and locally protected reserves have their own special regulations. Both general and specific information concerning these matters can be obtained at the natural park and tourist offices.

Long-distance trails (GR)

The renowned GR-11, which leads through the Spanish Pyrenees between the Mediterranean and the Atlantic, also touches on the walking regions of the Costa Brava. It begins (or ends) at the very very end of the Cap de Creus then turns inland near Llança through the Albera Natural Park and continues

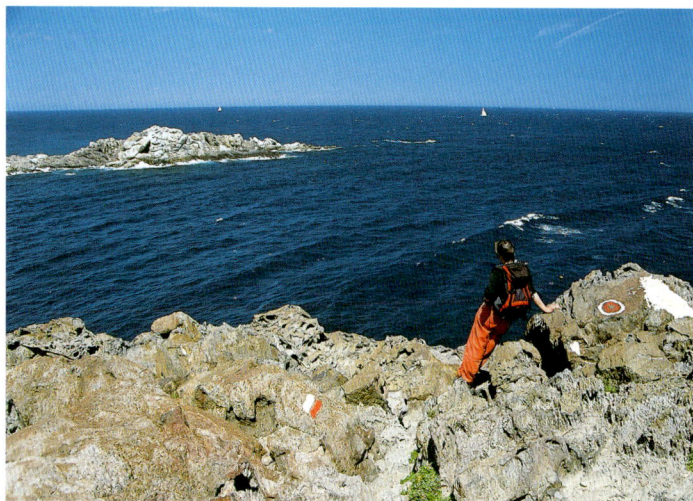

Cap de Creus: on Spain's easternmost promontory, the renowned GR-11 begins…or ends (Walk 22).

steadily at the foot of the Pyrenees' high ridge to La Jonquera. For the Costa Brava, the GR-92 is more relevant, running north to south from Portbou on the French border to Ulldecona on the southernmost end of Catalonia. This long-distance trail, also called the »Sendero Mediterráneo«, often leads directly along the seaboard and touches on numerous seaside villages. Many alternative routes fork off into the interior. While following the GR-92, a number of attractive combinations are possible, embracing the Catalonian regional trail (PR-C) as well as local walking trails so that a variety of supplementary excursions up hill and down dale can be worked out. The recently published GR-92 guide describes the course of the sections which can be trekked in a day: Sender de Gran Recorregut GR 92 (ed: Associació Catalana de Senderisme: serinfosender@euro-senders.com). Especially scenic landscapes along the GR-92 are the stretches between Llançà and Roses, L'Escala and Torroella de Montgrí as well as Begur and Tossa de Mar. The appealing GR-5, boasting a number of variations, is also worth mentioning: this long-distance trail leads through the interior and connects the Montserrat Mountains, Sant Llorenç del Munt i l'Obac and Montseny. For walkers wishing a more thorough exploration into the Montserrat region, the GR-172 is a good choice, offering nearly a complete circuit of the mountain.

Walking on the Costa Brava

The most varied of coastal landscapes on the Iberian Peninsula

Hardly any other region on the long Spanish coastline can compete with the Costa Brava in combining such a variety of natural landscapes. One cannot really speak of a prevailing type of scenery here; contrast is the key for the »wild coast« and its interior. Certainly the mountain regions near the coast belong to the range running from the eastern Pyrenees towards the south. Nevertheless, their outward appearance could hardly be more different. The whole spectrum is covered, from the volcanic hillocks near Olot to the conglomerate rock spires and needles of Montserrat before the gates of Barcelona, and from the granite ridges of the Muntanya de Verdera on the Cap de Creus to the beech-blanketed slopes of the Montseny. Between the Mediterranean-marked Pyrenees of the Alberas and the densely wooded Gavarres spread the expansive lowlands of the Empordà, intensively utilized for agricultural purposes – vineyards and rice cultivation among others. While most of the mountainous regions remain virtually unsettled or insignificantly so, along the narrower coast region, the northern and southern segments of the Costa Brava display conflicting images. Along the »wild« coast from Portbou to Tossa del Mar alternate vast stretches of undeveloped coastline and small towns and villages while the perfectly flat and dead straight seaboard from Blanes to Barcelona is densely populated and the sandy beaches found here are top-notch tourist attractions in summer. In contrast to this urban sprawl along the coastline, only a few kilometres away in the interior, three distinctly different mountain areas display completely different characteristics – the mountains of Montseny, Sant Llorenç del Munt i Serra de l'Obac and Montserrat. Together with several stretches of coastline and the Mediterranean Pyrenees, these regions enjoy the status of natural parks or nature reserves, through which their geological and scenic uniqueness – as well as the typical flora and fauna of the Costa Brava – is preserved and protected.

Flora and Fauna

The flora of the Costa Brava differs considerably from region to region and even within small areas, surprising contrasts in vegetation can be observed. The primordial, densely-wooded regions of the Pyrenees and the northern coast have virtually disappeared because of forest fires and logging and have given way to a Mediterranean scrub undergrowth dominated by broom, thyme, mastic shrub, lavender and rosemary. In contrast, mountainous regions like Montseny and Gavarres, as well as the volcanic terrain of the Garrotxa, remain dense woodland. Prevailing here are varieties of oak, beech and pine with some cork oaks and a shrinking number of rare species mixed in. The variety of blossoming plants is enormous, even in bleak and barren areas that appear desolate (like Cap de Creus or the limestone

A riot of flowers along the way to Cala Tavallera (Walk 21).

summits of Montgrí), a surprisingly wide range of colourfully blooming flowers, shrubs and bushes occur in spring and early summer.

In regards to fauna, mammals are very scarce indeed, although among the reptiles numerous types of lizards and snakes can be found. In contrast, birds and aquatic life-forms present a singular spectrum of species in the different regions. In the mountainous areas, depending on the rock formations and woodland found there, many different kinds of birds have made a home. The true paradise for birds, however, lies in the coastal regions in the north around Cap de Creus where innumerable seabirds and songbirds have settled down and migratory birds make their stopover. In the marshes of the Aiguamolls Nature Reserve on the Bay of Roses more than 320 species of birds have been recorded. The greatest variety of aquatic plants and animals can be found in the waters around the Cap de Creus and the Medes Islands offshore from L'Estartit. It is true that some organisms, including banks of precious coral, have been seriously decimated, but recent regulations to protect this coastal area have led to a rejuvenation of the endangered species.

Megalithic culture

At every turn, the walker is greeted by the earlier settlers of the Costa Brava through the presence of dolmen, menhire and burial sites. These stone relics from the late Neolithic period are particularly concentrated in the foothills of the Serra de l'Albera and in the hinterland of the Cap de Creus but also can be found on the southern seaboard. Most of these were erected between the 4th and the 2nd millennia BC and many have been discovered only fairly recently and faithfully reconstructed. In different regions »discovery trails« have been established to encourage visitors to these ancient cultural sites and often present attractive impressions of the natural landscape as well.

Menhir near Sant Onofre (Walk 17).

Natural parks & nature reserves

In the walking regions of the Costa Brava many mountain and coastal areas have obtained the status of natural parks or nature reserves. Special regulations regarding their use are in force in the protected zones.

Central information offices:

– Parc Natural de la Zona Volcànica de la Garrotxa
  El Casal dels Volcans in 17800 Olot, Av. de Santa Coloma, s/n. ✆ 972.26 62 02.
– Paratge Natural de l'Albera
  Rectoria Vella in 17753 Espolla, C.Amadeu Sudrià, 3. ✆ 972.545079.
– Parc Natural de Cap de Creus
  Casa de l'Abat in the Monestir de Sant Pere de Rodes, 17489 El Port de la Selva ✆ 972193191.
– Parc Natural Aiguamolls de l'Empordà
  El Cortalet (on the road to Sant Pere Pescador, km 13,6), 17486 Castelló d'Empúries. ✆ 972.454222.
– Parc Natural de Montseny
  Fontmartina (on the road from Sant Celoni to Turó de l'Home, km 10,8), 08470 Fogars de Montclus. ✆ 938.475102.
– Parc Natural de Sant Llorenç del Munt i l'Obac
  Centre d'Interpretació Coll d'Estenalles (on the BV-1221 between Terrassa and Navarcles, km 14,8) ✆ 938.317300.
– Parc Natural del Montserrat
  Oficina de Turisme, Plaça de la Creu, 08199 Monestir de Montserrat. ✆ 938.777777.

Swimming

Of course, the Costa Brava is a paradise for bathing fans. Exceptions to the rule are some steep stretches of coastline where hidden bays can only be reached by boat. Other than these, the coast offers numerous opportunities for bathing, to satisfy every fancy, from mile-long expanses of sandy beach through to remote protected coves only accessible along steep footpaths.

Canyoning

In the mountainous interior of the Costa Brava and in the nearby Pyrenees, fans of this wet adventure sport will surely get their money's worth. The most beautiful gorge for this experience is the Gorga de Sant Aniol (not far from Olot) and can be combined with the neighbouring Gorga de Les Canals. Information on guided canyoning tours and outfitters can be obtained at the local tourist offices.

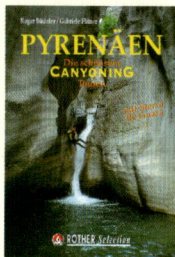

Paragliding

One of the preferred areas for paragliding is the Cap de Creus. The peninsula provides just the right conditions. Promoters of the sport can be found in El Port de la Selva and Roses.

Rock-climbing

An outstanding attraction for rock-climber visiting the Costa Brava is the Montserrat Natural Park near Barcelona. In this bizarre massif of conglomerate rock crags, numerous routes in every grade of difficulty have been established, and can be clambered year-round. In summer, the shady north side is the most popular area. For rock-climbers living in Barcelona, Montserrat is the native mountain so there is plenty of company at the weekend. Good rock-climbing can also be had in Sant Llorenç del Munt i l'Obac Natural Park north of Terrassa.

Mountain biking and cycling

Cycling enthusiasts, especially those with a good deal of training, will find a good selection of tracks as well as mountain and coastal roads to challenge them. Individual regions are covered in detail by published guides and most tourist offices provide brochures with suggested routes. The prettiest stretch of coast for the cyclist is the road GI-682 between Sant Feliu de Guíxols and Lloret de Mar.

Sailing and surfing

The Costa Brava is an eldorado for sailing and windsurfing. In addition to superb conditions for these water sports, one can find idyllic harbours and isolated anchorages not possible to reach by land.

The windsurfer will be challenged by every grade of difficulty when it comes to wind and wave. Water sport clubs are located in practically every coastal community.

Diving

Following the establishment of strict regulations regarding environmental protection, the underwater world has clearly become more and more attractive for diving and snorkelling. The most popular diving grounds are found at Cap de Creus and the Illes Medes off of L'Estartit. Diving schools are available everywhere along the coast.

Information and addresses

Getting there
The Costa Brava can be reached by car either by driving the panoramic road along the coast from Perpignan to Cerbère and Portbou or, more quickly, via the motorway or the main road over the Coll del Pertús to Figueres. The rail journey along the seaboard from Perpignan is also a comfortable option. Barcelona is the main hub for all of the international airlines but service has also picked up to Girona, mostly by charter airlines and airlines specializing in cheap fares.

Information & brochures
Local tourist offices are cited in the key point section prefacing the individual walk descriptions. Since office hours are rarely consistent, so place a telephone call before paying a visit.
Main tourist offices:
Great Britain: Spanish Tourist Office, 22-23 Manchester Square, London WIU 3PX, ✆ +44 207 4868077, www.tourspain.co.uk, e-mail: info.londres@tourspain.es; Canada: Spanish Tourist Office, Bloor Street West 2 – Suite 3402, Ontario – M4W 3E2 Toronto, ✆ +1 416 9613131, www.tourspain.toronto.on.ca, e-mail: Toronto@tourspain.es; USA: Tourist Office of Spain, 666 Fifth Avenue, 35th floor, New York, NY 10103, ✆ +1 212 2658822, Fax: +1 212 2658864, e-mail: oetny@tourspain.es; Barcelona (Centre d'Informació Turística de Catalunya): Passeig de Gràcia, 105; ✆ 932.384000; Girona: Rambla de la Llibertat, 1; ✆ 972.226575; Figueres: Plaça del Sol: ✆ 972. 503155; Olot: C/Hospici, 8; ✆ 972.260141; La Bispal d'Empordà: Plaça del Castell; ✆ 972.642593.

For a regularly updated list of internet links, try the website of the Bergverlag Rother: www.rother.de (WebLinks/GeoLinks).

Mountaineering club
The Catalonian section of the Spanish Mountaineering Club is the Federació d'Entitats Excursionistes de Catalunya (FEEC), Rambla 41, 08002 Barcelona; ✆ 93.4120777. www.feec.es

Festivals
From the capital city to the smallest Catalonian hamlet, festivals (fiestas) are a vital part of traditional Spanish life, with communities observing many local customs and rituals. Several music and dance festivals, often performed in front of impressive stage sets, have achieved international fame. The Catalonian Festival Schedule lists fiestas for the whole year round; traditional village galas are most frequent in the high season. Tourist offices provide up-to-date listings of the festivals taking place.

Opening hours

As a rule, shops are open as follows: 10am – 1pm, then 4:30pm – 7:30pm (Mon – Sat); only bakeries are open on Sunday. These normal opening hours vary considerably depending on the season and the kind of business. The larger supermarkets on the edges of town are often open without a pause, sometimes even on Sunday. Banks and post offices are open from 9am – 2pm, Monday to Friday.

Climate

The mild and temperate Mediterranean climate of the Costa Brava is marked by stable weather conditions in winter and summer, often with long periods of high pressure and sunshine. The region's proximity to the Mediterranean, the blocking effect of the Pyrenees to the north, and its position set apart from the influence of Atlantic low pressure systems are important factors in determining temperatures and yearly averages of sunny and rainy days. The lowest average temperatures occur between December and March, although December and January can still boast almost 60% of days with sunshine. The most pleasant temperatures are experienced from April to June and in September and October; the highest temperatures are in July and August when the average maximum reaches 26°C. In summer, strong winds from the interior and the sea breeze provide a noticeable cooling effect. Most rainfall occurs in autumn and in spring. At these times, one can expect sudden, severe changes in the weather, often accompanied by thunderstorms and, in the higher mountain areas, by snowfall. A typical feature of the northern Costa Brava is the tramuntana. This inland wind origi-

A windswept pine on the Cap de Norfeu (Walk 23).

nates in the French Roussillon, gusts over the Pyrenees and can easily reach speeds of over 120km an hour. Since it is usually called forth by a high pressure area building up over the Iberian Peninsula, the tramuntana sweeps in during sunny weather from a north or north-westerly direction, blasting the Costa Brava. In the cooler seasons it can become a dry, cold storm. The Cap de Creus suffers the most from this wind as a result of its obstructing location. Normally, the wind dies down in two or three days.

Emergency and rescue
The general emergency number is: ✆ 112. The local fire brigade (Bombers) is in charge of mountain rescue: ✆ 085.

Accommodation
Hotels, pensions and campsites of all categories can be found in profusion all over the Costa Brava. Accommodation guides for the different regions are readily available at the tourist offices. Youth hostels can be found in many of the larger settlements in the interior and are without age restrictions in Spain, however, a membership fee must be paid. It has become increasingly popular to stay in turismo rural and in residències-casa de pagès (CP) accommodation: rooms, apartments or separate cottages on country estates or private property in the countryside. An informal atmosphere in a scenic location, often accompanied by excellent cuisine, makes such lodgings especially attractive. The Catalonian Government (Generalitat de Catalunya) Department of Tourism publishes a yearly guide for the CP which can also be placed on order. A list of accommodation falling under

Forest fire site in the St. Llorenc del Munt Natural Park.

the framework of turismo rural is available on the internet under www.catalunya.net and www.turismerural.com.

Danger of forest fire

Forest fires are a virulent danger on the entire Costa Brava and in the densely wooded interior near the coast, especially in the dry summer months and during high winds. While in days gone by, fires were purposely set to clear land for agriculture or construction, nowadays carelessness is the usual cause of forest fire. Just recently, in the summer of 2003, a number of different woodlands of the Costa Brava – including natural parks – were plagued by disastrous fires that even threatened hamlets and villages. Forest fires can often destroy vast areas of valuable woodland and natural vegetation as well as precious wildlife. Since the mountainous regions and natural parks are provided with only a few access roads, it is extremely difficult to keep fires under control.

Conscientious conduct and absolute adherence to relevant regulations are called for to avoid forest fires. Please consult local tourist offices for information concerning the currently valid rules of conduct.

Websites

Information about the walking regions, as well as accommodation, activities, festivals, nature, culture, weather, villages etc. can be found under: www.costabrava.org / www.gencat.es / www.cbrava.es / www.pirineos.com

Trails

A well-developed, maintained and marked system of walking trails encompasses the Costa Brava's most beautiful regions and routes. A »Camí de Ronda« (literally: circular trail) is typically found in the coastal regions. These trails, established for ramblers and walkers by the individual communities, usually lead directly along the seaside over cliffs and beaches, also often through settled areas. The »sender local« is a local white/green marked walking trail that is conceived as an easily manageable day trip.

The white/yellow marked PR-C is a long-distance trail special to Catalonia and established for longer stretches, but is ideal for day trips and for combinations using local walking trails. Since this walking trail often crosses or even shares the course of the GR long-distance trails, a tight and variable walking network prevails.

Weather forecasts

Tourist offices issue up-to-the-minute daily weather forecasts. For information over the telephone, call the Instituto Nacional de Meteorologia ℭ 906.365325; www.inm.es.

Weather forecasts for specific regions can be found at the Servei de meteorologia de Catalunya website; www.gencat.es/servmet.

Map — Catalonia / Pyrenees region

Cities and towns:
Puigcerdà, Camprodon, Ribes de Freser, Ripoll, Berga, Torelló, Manlleu, Vic, Cardona, Súria, Manresa, Sabadell, Terrassa, Granollers, Cardedeu, Sallent, Navàs, Moià, Centelles, Tona, Olesa, Esparreguera, Mollet

Place names (north area):
el Barida, Aranser, Aristot, Toloriu, Arseguel, Estana, Prullans, Lles de Cerdanya, Martinet, Bellver de Cerdanya, Das, Prats, Brus, Tossa, Montellà, la Molina, Alp, Astoll, Ger, Bolvir, Vilallobent, Queixans, Urtx, Pi, Isovol, Guils de Cerdanya, Meranges, Baixa Cerdanya, Enveig, Llívia, Estavar, Gorguja, Saillagouse, Ste-Leocadie, Eyne, Err, Planes, Bains, Odeillo-Via, Targassonne, Dorres, Font-Romeu, les Cabanasse, les Estables, la Cabanasse

Central area:
Montellà de Cadí, Bagà, Guardiola de Berguedà, Monast. de Saldes, Saldes, Gósol, Palomera, Vallcebre, Figols, Castellar del Riu, Ntra. Sra. de Queralt, Peguera, Cercs, Vilada, Borreda, Avià, Olvan, Gironella, Els Bassacs, Casserres, Montclar, Capolat, l'Espunyola, Puig-reig, Viver, Serrateix, Cal Riera, Gaià, Balsareny, Avinyó, Artés, Calders, Santa Maria d'Oló, l'Estany

Ripollès area:
Molló, Vilallonga de Ter, Setcases, Tregurà de Dalt, Llanars, Pardines, Planoles, Toses, Nava, Campelles, Queralbs, Núria, Bruguera, Ogassa, St. Joan de les Abadesses, Sant Pau de Segúries, Camprodon, Joanetes, els Hostalets d'en Bas, St. Privat d'en Bas, Sant Pere de Torelló, St. Vicenç de Torelló, Ntra. Sra. de Bellmunt, Sant Quirze de Besora, Santa Maria de Besora, Montesquiu, Sora, la Farga de Bebié, les Llosses, Palmerola, Matamala, Campdevànol, St. Quirze de Besora

Osona area:
Sant Agustí de Lluçanès, Sant Boi de Lluçanès, Perafita, Sobremunt, Sant Hipòlit de Voltregà, Sant Martí d'Albars, Olost, Prats de Lluçanès, St. Feliu Sasserra, Oristà, Sta. Maria de Merlès, Sant Bartomeu del Grau, Gurb, Tavèrnoles, Roda de Ter, Sant Pere de Casserres, Taradell, Viladrau, Seva, el Brull, Folgueroles, Calldetenes, St. Julià de Vilatorta, St. Sadurní d'Osormort, Espinelves, Malla, St. Eulàlia de Riuprimer, St. Eugènia de Berga, Muntanyola

South area:
Súria, Callús, Santpedor, St. Joan de Vilatorrada, St. Fruitós de Bages, Navarcles, Talamanca, Mura, Sant Llorenç Savall, Monistrol de Calders, Castellterçol, Granera, Sant Quirze Safaja, Gallifa, Sant Feliu de Codines, l'Ametlla del Vallès, Bigues, Riells, Figaró, Montmany, St. Feliu del Racó, Castellar del Vallès, Sentmenat, Matadepera, Vacarisses, Monistrol de Montserrat, Castellbell i el Vilar, El Pont de Vilomara, St. Vicenç de Castellet, Castellgalí, Sant Salvador de Guardiola, Castellfollit del Boix, Rellinars, Viladecavalls, Vallès Occidental, La Garriga, Cardedeu, St. Antoni de Vilamajor, St. Pere de Vilamajor, Palautordera, Sta. Maria de Palautordera, Montseny, la Roca del Vallès, Argentona, Cabrils, Orrius, Vilanova del Vallès, Montornès, Parets del Vallès, Palau-solità i Plegamans, Lliçà d'Amunt, Lliçà de Vall, Polinyà, St. Perpètua de Mogoda, Caldes de Montbui, Sentmenat, Castellterçol

Other:
la Coma, Sant Llorenç de Morunys, Castelltallat, Olius, Pegueroles, Naves, St. Susanna, Castelladral, Pinós, Vallmanya, Su, Gironella, Cal Rosal

Terrassa, Sabadell, Mollet del Vallès, Montmeló, Argentona

Esparreguera, Olesa de Montserrat, El Bruc, Collbató, Monistrol de Montserrat, Montserrat, La Pobla de Claramunt, Igualada, Òdena, Jorba, Castellolí, Vilanova del Camí

Numbered markers: 15, 22, 18, 25, 17, 53, 80, 30, 45, 1-3, 5, 32, 74, 60, 38, 36, 37, 39, 41, 42, 44, 45, 43, 40, 20, 46-50, 54, 18, 22, 10-23

Céret
lie-les-Bains
Palalda
Arles-sur-Tech
Montalba-d'Amélie
St-Laurent-de-Cerdans
Coustouges
Tapis
Maçanet de Cabrenys
Darnius
la Vajol
Agullana
la Jonquera
Cantallops
Requeseris
sa de l'Albe
Portbou
Colera
Portbou
St-Quirze de Colera
Vilamaniscle
Llança
el Port de la Selva
la Selva de Mar
cap de Creus
Port-Lligat
Cadaqués
St Climent Sescebes
Campmany
Masarac
Garriguella
Vilajuiga
Pau
Palau-Saverdera
Vilanova de la Muga
Peralada
Marza
Roses
Cap Norfeu
Montalba
Boadella
la Guardia de Molins
Terrades
Vilarig
Pont de Molins
Llers
Cabanes
Vilabertran
Figueres
Vila-Sacra
Castelló d'Empúries
Fortia
Ruimors
Sta Bomba
Castell de St Ferran
Avinyonet de Puigventós
Vilafant
Vilamalla
Vilacolum
St Pere Pescador
l'Armentera
Borrassà
Siurana
Toroella de Fluvià
Ventalló
Montiró
Albanyà
Ntra. Sra. del Mont
St Martí Sesserres
Beuda
Cabanelles
Mata de Montcal
Navata
Ordis
St Miquel de Fluvià
St Mori
Viladamat
Albons
Montgó
l'Escala
Bellcaire
la Tallada
Verges
la Bisbal d'Empordà
Palafrugell
Begur
Cap de Begur
Fornells de Mar
Aiguablava
Cova del Bisbe
Llafranc
Castella de Palafrugell
Calella
Tamariu
Regencós
Pals
Pineda
Riera
Cap de la Barra
Illes Medes
l'Estartit
Torroella de Montgrí
els Masos de Pals
Dunas
Besalú
el Torn
Serinyà
St Miquel de Campmajor
Porqueres
Banyoles
Mieres
St Aniol de Finestres
St Esteve de Llémena
Cornellà de Terri
Palol de Revardit
Ma Mota
St Jordi Desvalls
Cervià de Ter
Bordils
Flaçà
Sant Julià de Ramis
Celrà
St Martí Vell
GIRONA / GERONA
Sarrià de Ter
Sant Gregori
Bescanó
Vilablareix
Aiguaviva
Anglès
Brunyola
St Coloma de Farners
Riudellots de la Selva
Fornells de la Selva
Cassà de la Selva
Llambilles
Quart
St Mateu de Montnegre
St Sadurní de l'Heura
Cruïlles
Monells
Vulpellac
Peratallada
Ullastret
Corçà
Madremanya
Sant Feliu de Guíxols
Platja d'Aro
Castell d'Aro
Calonge
Sant Antoni de Calonge
Palamós
Vall-Llobrega
Mont-ras
Llofriu
Castell
Punta Prava
S'Agaró
Canyet de Mar
Santa Cristina
Tossa de Mar
Cap de Tossa
Lloret de Mar
Blanes
Llagostera
Caldes de Malavella
Sant Llorenç
St Seclina
St Grau
Riudarenes
Massanes
Hostalric
Maçanet de la Selva
Sils
Vidreres
Tordera
Palafolls
Malgrat de Mar
Pineda de Mar
Sant Pol de Mar
Canet de Mar
Arenys de Mar
Calella
St Cebrià de Vallalta

The environs of Olot

»Volcanic« in the usual sense of the word hardly matches the landscape of the »Zona Volcànica de la Garrotxa« east of Olot. The densely wooded summits rise up only a few hundred metres from the surrounding countryside, a fine counterpoise to the Pyrenees chain on the horizon. Nonetheless, the area is of true volcanic origin – geologically speaking, somewhat strange since it belongs to the mountain network of the Serralada Transversal range, which connects the Pyrenees to the low mountain massif of the Montseny Natural Park south of Girona. An eccentric, one could say. At least thirty volcanic cones and craters have retained their appearance after the extinction of their volatility. The last eruption occurred 11,500 years ago at El Croscat, one of the most important volcanoes of the region apart from Santa Margarida (Walk 4). Things have been quiet since; the volcanoes are now popular tourist attractions. Natural landscapes like these are rare on the Iberian Peninsula, so in 1985 – initiatives seeking to protect the area go back to 1917! – the Catalonian government designated the area a »Parc Natural«. The natural park actually encloses an area of 12,000 hectares, and a carefully-maintained network of tracks allows for almost boundless exploration. A curious feature is the lush flora dominating the landscape, stimulated by relatively high precipitation and warm temperatures. This damp habitat allows many varieties of flora to flourish and even produces endemic species like the Pyrenean violet and the Pyrenean saxifrage. Rightfully respected and renowned, the dense forests of the natural park consist mostly of oak and beech trees. These blanket the slopes of the volcanic cones and craters to bestow the scenery with a vivid

The striking basalt columns of Sant Joan les Fonts (Walk 1).

The Cingles near Rupit (Walk 6).

shade of green that so effectively sets off the snow-whiteness of Canigou in springtime.

Another counterpoise to the volcanic landscape rises up to the south-west of Olot – the pre-Pyrenean Puigsacalm Massif (Walks 1-3), a rugged mountain range towering over the lovely hamlets of Sant Privat d'en Bas and Joanetes. This eye-catching prominence also offers a superlative viewing point and is a very popular walking excursion for the Catalonians. The viewing point can be approached from a number of directions; the north face presents the most difficult one but also has a lot to offer: the fascinating Salt de Sallent waterfall, the »Mare de Déu de les Ollettes« chapel built into a cliff face and the little church of »Santa Magdalena de Mont«, fantastically and panoramically situated on a cliff top. The long tradition of chapels and hermitages is also omnipresent in the Pyrenean foothills north of the Fluvià Valley, inevitably at the most beautiful locations and where the most spectacular views are taken in. Countless »Ermitas« can be reached by trails leading through delightful natural scenery, and also provide lovely spots to take a break while storming a summit, e.g. along the route to Roc de Frausa near Maçanet de Cabrenys (Walk 7). The highest peak of the chain between Coll d'Ares and the Mediterranean is a brilliant viewing point amidst the Mediterranean pasturelands of the Alt Empordà and the magnificent Massif de Canigou facing opposite.

North-east of Vic, between the Puigsacalm Mountains and the grand reservoirs of the Río Ter, steep, high plateaux rise up to the heavens. The so-called Cingles (Walks 5 and 6) dominate the scene with striking cliff faces; the expansive cliff tops offer spectacular panoramic walks, easily combined with visits to the scattered, quaint villages of the area.

1   Puigsacalm, 1514m

A Catalonian summit – the easy way around

Collada de Bracons – Rasos de Manter – Puigsacalm and back

Starting point: Collada de Bracons, 1132m. From Olot drive south on the C-153; past Les Preses, turn right onto the BV 5224 climbing to the pass. There are little lay-bys for parking here.

Walking times: Collada de Bracons – Rasos de Manter 1¼ hrs, Rasos de Manter – Puigsacalm ½ hr, return 1½ hrs; total time 3¼ hrs.

Ascent: 382m.

Grade: Not a difficult walk with mostly easy ascents.

Trail markings: Blue/red (sometimes faded).

Refreshment: None en route; Joanetes.

Map: Puigsacalm-Bellmunt, 1:25,000 (Editorial Alpina).

Info: Oficina de Turisme in Les Preses; ✆ 972.692020.

Tip: The basalt columns at Sant Joan les Fonts. Starting on the north side of the Plaça Major, not far from the BBVA-Bank and at numerous road signs – one with »Columnes Basàltiques« – a narrow street turns off. Take this to the stone bridge crossing the river then continue on the trail »Ruta de les 3 Colades« (no.16) passing on the eastern side of the church, behind which an excursion can be made (sign »Molí Fondo«) by de-

scending to the riverbank formed by layers of lava. Turn back and head for »Cingles«. Near a house, ascend along a tarmac road for 50m then turn right at the trail sign. At the following fork, continue straight on until meeting a track. Turn right and descend until almost reaching the level of the river. Now head upriver and end at a wide cliff face of basalt columns (sign »Cingles«) to the left of the trail (total time 1½ hrs).

A unique view sweeping all points of the compass makes the Puigsacalm an extraordinary destination for mountaineers in the Catalonian foothills of the Pyrenees. At the weekend, walkers ascend from all directions along trails that clearly differ from each other in length and grade. The approach road from the Collada de Bracons is the easiest and most frequented stretch of trail, though lacking nothing in scenic beauty. The viewing point from the summit is then shared by everybody.

On the **Collada de Bracons** turn northwards and climb up the rocky embankment of the roadside, following red arrow markings. Ascend to a large wooden post where the trail begins with a steep, strenuous climb. Immedi-

View of the Pyrenees chain from Puigsacalm.

ately after, continue on an easy up-and-down path through the lovely beech forest on the western slopes to reach the Collada de Sant Bartomeu, 1249m. The tiny pass is marked by a narrow passage through the rock, blocked by a cable, behind which the trail forks off in a number of directions. Here, turn sharply to the right (numerous markings). Immediately after, the trail leads past a beech tree with »Font« written on it in red. Continue on, walking pleasantly up and down, until reaching a fork where the walking trail from Vidrà merges. Head for »Font Tornadissa« and »Puigsacalm« to the right, and soon meet up with burly beech trees enclosing the spring. Here, the path ascends along a stretch of thinly-wooded slope and towards a clearly visible solitary box tree. At the same time, a trail marking in the form of a wooden post appears. Bear to the right here and ascend along the gentle ridge following even more wooden posts to the **Rasos de Manter**, 1389m (sign). Now turn right toward »Puigsacalm« and continue on, following the fence. At the end, pass through a wooden gate. Along a distinct trail, pass over a small saddle and then cross open terrain until entering another beech wood. Here at the foot of the summit and the beginning of the final ascent, the trail forks (a first-aid kit has been attached to a tree at this point). Head straight on and ascend along a washed-out trail until reaching the **Puigsacalm**, 1514m.

2   Salt de Sallent, 1020m

Circular walk around a splendid waterfall

Sant Privat d'en Bas – Salt de Sallent and back

Starting point: Picnic grounds on the Río Gurn near Sant Privat d'en Bas, 530m. From Olot drive south on the C-153; in Les Preses turn right onto the GIP-5226 towards Sant Privat d'en Bas, shortly before reaching the village and next to a power station, turn left onto the track (signed; e.g. »Salt de Sallent«) until reaching another fork, then turn right and down to the »Zona de Pícnic« at the stream.

Walking times: Picnic grounds – Salt de Sallent 1½ hrs, return 1¼ hrs; total time 2¾ hrs.

Ascent: 490m.

Grade: Fairly strenuous stretches of ascent and descent.

Trail markings: Sometimes wooden posts with trail signs.

Refreshment: None en route; restaurant »Can Turó« ; Sant Privat d'en Bas.

Map: Puigsacalm-Bellmunt, 1:25,000 (Editorial Alpina).

Info: Oficina de Turisme in Sant Privat d'en Bas; ✆ 972.692177.

Tip: Competent canyonists will find the descent from the Salt de Sallent a first-class technical challenge and a scenic one. Absolute mastery of abseil technique is required. Rope lengths: 2 × 60m. Belaying anchors at the starting point orographically left of the rock rim below the tree; tricky access. For description and topography refer to E.Gómez: Descenso de Cañones. GIRONA (tomo II).

The Riera de Sallent murmurs placidly through a meadow on a plateau then suddenly disappears over a sheer rock edge and into the void. That is how the Salt de Sallent appears from above. The approach from below reveals the complimentary picture: a wide, almost sheer cliff face, beautiful in itself,

The sensational, plunging Salt de Sallent.

where the stream drops down as a shower of raindrops. The walk around the Salt del Sallent is very attractive with an impressive natural landscape and a shady picnic place on the banks of the stream.

From the car park at the **picnic grounds**, climb left to the forestry road. Here, turn right and at the same time pass by a road forking left (»Can Turó«). Also ignore the next signed fork along the »Camí dels Matxos« – this trail will serve for the descent from the Salt de Sallent. Instead, continue straight ahead towards »Salt de Sallent per les escales« and soon the wide, colourful cliff with the waterfall comes into view. At a wooden post with a green sign, leave the road by turning left and follow the delightful trail through a dense mixed forest along the Río Gurn. On the way, cross over two tributary streams, then the trail reaches the main stream. Cross to the other side over numerous boulders and then begin a very strenuous climb through steep slopes. In an ingeniously plotted ascent, the »escales« – literally »steps« – wind along the seemingly insurmountable cliff face, helped by spanned cables on some of the steeper stretches. Once at the top, reach open woodland and soft rolling meadows. Pass by a gate and, at the signed trail crossing, bear left (bearing right leads to Vidrá). Enjoying a lovely view of the steep cliff faces and into the far distance, continue on to the meandering stream that suddenly plunges more than 100m into the deep at the cliff's edge of the **Salt de Sallent**, 1020m. Watch out, there's no real foothold at the edge!

Cross over the stream and follow the trail on the other side – this immediately leads over a tributary stream and then merges with an old track. Here, turn left. At the sign for »Sant Privat« turn left to leave the track (this continues on to the chapel Santa Magdalena de Mont → Walk 3) and begin a descent through dense forest. This glorious trail soon crosses over a brook. Ignore a trail to the right marked by cairns then take a bend into a side valley with a gully, filled with massive boulders, dropping downwards. The trail crosses over the blockaded valley floor, then turns again down the valley and becomes an old track that soon takes an abrupt left-hand bend. In the bend, at a wooden signpost, a trail forks to the right and leads in a steep descent to the picnic grounds. Remain, however, on the pleasant track to join up again with the road leading through the little valley of the Río Gurn. Turn right onto this to return to the **picnic grounds**.

3   Northern ascent to Puigsacalm, 1514m

Superlative scenery in the foothills of the Pyrenees

Sant Privat d'en Bas – Santa Magdalena de Mont – Puigsacalm and back

Starting point: Picnic grounds on the Río Gurn near Sant Privat d'en Bas, 530m.
From Olot head south on the C-153; in Les Preses turn right onto the GIP-5226 towards Sant Privat d'en Bas, shortly before reaching the village and next to a power station, turn left onto the track (signed; e.g. »Salt de Sallent«) until reaching another fork, then turn right and down to the »Zona de Pícnic« at the stream.

Walking times: Picnic grounds – Santa Magdalena del Mont 1¾ hrs, Santa Magdalena del Mont – Puigsacalm ¾ hr, return 2 hrs; total time 4½ hrs.

Ascent: 945m.

Grade: A long walk with demanding differences in height and very strenuous ascents.

Trail markings: Some stretches with signed wooden posts; ascent to the Puigsacalm with red markings.

Refreshment: None en route; restaurant »Can Turó«, Sant Privat d'en Bas.

Map: Puigsacalm-Bellmunt, 1:25,000 (Editorial Alpina).

Info: Oficina de Turisme in Sant Privat d'en Bas; ✆ 972.692177.

Possible combination: With Walk 2 via the Salt de Sallent.

Tip: The »volcano« town of Olot, where scenic, historical and architectural aspects have been bound together along a circular route for visitors.

The ascent along the steep northern slopes to the Puigsacalm offers a grandiose panoramic view of this very popular mountain. In addition, on the shady trail leading up to the peak lies the little chapel of Mare de Déu de les Olletes built into a cliff face, and further up is an enticing excursion to the chapel of Santa Magdalena del Mont, built on a projecting plateau high above the Bas Valley. This is a wonderful place to take a break before accomplishing the final push to the peak. For the walker still looking for adventure, another excursion can be added to view the impressive plunging waterfall Salt de Sallent on the return route.

From the **picnic grounds** head for the road, bearing right until reaching the junction marked with large trail signs. Take the left-hand fork for the road towards »Puigsacalm« and soon arrive at Can Turó. Here, pass through the archway of the restaurant and start off at the trail head with the signpost at the open-air terrace. After a long, strenuous, steep ascent through the pleasant wood, meet up with a signed junction: the left fork points to Joanetes but bear right to continue towards »Puigsacalm«. Along a level stretch of trail, reach the cliff grotto of Mare de Déu de les Ollettes with a statue of the Virgin Mary. Immediately after, the trail ascends at a rapid pace and winds along a steep stream gully climbing through a densely wooded slope. Turn left at the marked forestry road. Pass by a small spring nestled under a burly beech tree on the left-hand side of the trail (sign »Font«), and a few minutes later reach the chapel of **Santa Magdalena de Mont**, 1280m, marvellously situated against its mountainous Pyrenean backdrop. A part of the building has been set aside as a *refugí*.

Walk back to the forestry track junction and follow the sign »Puigsacalm« by bearing diagonally left and, after a short stretch of trail

Santa Magdalena de Mont chapel.

through a beech wood with some scattered box trees, reach a trail junction. On the left hand side the »Camí dels Burros« forks off but bear right along a path leading through the steep slopes of the Puig dels Llops, a secondary peak to the north-east of the Puigsacalm. The ascent is trail-marked on trees in red and climbs steeply through densely wooded slopes. The path then winds southwards to reach an open beech wood. To the left is a possible excursion to the Puig dels Llops, 1486m. Continue straight on in a south-westerly direction through the wood to meet up with the trail approaching from the Rasos de Manter (→ Walk 1). Turn left here (sign »Puigsacalm«) and follow the well-trodden, rutted trail climbing steeply to **Puigsacalm**, 1514m.

4 The »Zona Volcànica« near Olot

Circular route in the volcanic natural park

Àrea de Santa Margarida – Volcà de Santa Margarida – Fageda d'en Jordà – Grederes Volcà del Croscat – Àrea de Santa Margarida

Starting point: The car park Àrea de Santa Margarida, 560m. From Olot along the GI-524, a little past km 6.

Walking times: Àrea de Santa Margarida – Volcà de Santa Margarida ½ hr, Volcà de Santa Margarida – Fageda d'en Jordà 1½ hrs, Fageda d'en Jordà – Grederes del Volcà del Croscat 1½ hrs, Grederes del Volcà del Croscat – Àrea de Santa Margarida ½ hr; total time 4 hrs.

Ascent: About 400m.

Grade: Although longer, overall an uncomplicated walk.

Markings: Natural park trail (Itinerari 1); red diamonds on wooden posts.

Refreshment: None en route; Santa Pau.

Map: Zona Volcànica de la Garrotxa, 1:30,000 (ICC).

Info: Information centre for the Can Serra Natural Park on the GI-524 near km 4; ☎ 972.195074 as well as Can Passavent near the El Croscat volcano; ☎ 972.195094. Both information centres are located along the way.

Tip: The volcano museum in Olot: Casal dels Volcans, Av. Santa Coloma, 43; ☎ 972.266762. Open daily (except Tuesday) 10 am – 2 pm and 4 pm – 6 pm; on holidays, only open in the morning.

A geological curiosity: only a few kilometres from the central axis of the Pyrenees lies a small volcanic area with numerous volcanic domes, many of these even within the nearby city limits of Olot. In the excellently preserved natural park »Zona Volcànica de la Garrotxa« many hiking trails have been established, but this circular route shows the various physical features of the area in the best way.

At the **Àrea de Santa Margarida**, the trail begins near the information board and follows the sign in the direction »Volcà de Santa Margarida«. The wide track ascends through woodland. At the fork immediately following, bear right towards »Crater de Volcà«. The trail passes by a farmstead and then ascends to the crater rim of the **Volcà de Santa Margarida**, 760m. The chapel of the same name has been built on the floor of the crater; directly before or behind the Can Santa, descending trails can be taken for a visit there. Continue, however, along the same trail towards »Sant Miquel de Sacot«. Near a trail marking and a sign »No pasar« a forest path breaks off left to circle the volcano along the crater's rim, but descend instead along the forestry road through a holm oak wood to reach a junction. Turn right here to follow the white/red marked GR-2. At the fork immediately following, bear right again and continue above the terraced basin until reaching signposts. Here, leave the forestry road behind and descend into the basin. Turn right onto a tarmac road and follow this for a short way, then turn left onto a signed short-cut that returns to the road. This ascends to the beautifully-situated little church of Sant Miquel de Sacot. Another 50m along the tar-

Pyroclastic cone.

mac road, turn right by the sign »Fageda d'en Jordà«. The sometimes deeply-rutted trail later widens into a track along the Prat de la Plaça. At the end of the grassy plain, near a large farmstead, the track merges with a tarmac road. Turn right to continue, pass the large Cooperativa and reach a property with a small hut enclosed by a dry stone wall. Ignoring the trail forking right to »Can Xel«, reach another junction 50m further on – the GR and the Itinerari no.3 fork left here. Instead, continue along the road for a short way then turn left onto the signed forest trail to the **Fageda d'en Jordà**, 570m.

Surrounded by the beautiful beech wood, follow the trail until reaching the road where a pedestrian tunnel crosses over to the information centre »Can Serra«. At the signposts there, follow the direction »Grederes Volcà del Croscat«, walking through a wood and then meeting up with a track to the left. Turn left to follow this track along the foot of the wooded slopes of the volcano, passing clearings in the wood of exposed volcanic rock, until ending at a road. Turn right here and after a few steps, turn sharp right onto the gated road ascending to the information centre »Can Passavent«. From there, the green-marked Itinerari no.15 leads to the **Grederes del Volcà del Croscat**, 680m, where volcanic rock was once quarried. The large exposure stretches to the very summit of the volcano where an old watchtower is perched.

After taking a little circular trail to admire the striking geological features, return to Can Passavent. Now follow the signed path »Aparcament Sta. Margarida«. This leads through a little holm oak wood and then drops down to the road. Turn right to reach the GI-524, then left for a short stretch and finally cross over to the **Àrea de Santa Margarida**.

5 On the Cingles d'Aiats, 1290m

The table-top mountains of Cantonigròs

Pont de la Rotllada – Pla d'Aiats – Pont de la Rotllada

Starting point: Pont de la Rotllada, 900m; km 23,5 on the C-135 between Roda de Ter and Rupit.
Walking times: Pont de la Rotllada – Pla d'Aiats 1¾ hrs, Pla d'Aiats – Pont de la Rotllada 1¼ hrs; total time 3 hrs.
Ascent: About 390m.
Grade: Sure-footedness and some sense of direction are required for the return route; the descent is sometimes steep.
Trail markings: Blue trail markings, sometimes faded, few and far between.
Refreshment: None en route; Cantonigròs.
Map: El Collsacabra, 1:25,000 (Editorial Piolet).
Info: Information centre in Rupit; ✆ 938.522083.
Notice: The 1.3 km long track could be driven to the fork for the Aiats farmstead, however, parking places are few.
Tip: A visit to Vic. The capital city of the Osona Province sports a splendid old town centre and an »Italian«-style Plaça Major. A signed circular route (Ruta

turística) leads past numerous interesting tourist sites.

Cingles – this is the name given to the rock faces dropping sheerly from flat high ridges. The mesa-like limestone heights characterize the landscape north of the Río Ter reservoirs and provide myriad walks with commanding views. The circular walk along the Cingles of Aiats combines ascents and descents through delightful forests with enjoyable rambling along the panoramic high plateau.

At the **Pont de la Rotllada**, the walk begins along the track towards »Caselles« and »Aiats«. Continue straight on at the fork to the Caselles farmstead and then reach another junction with a trail sign: the track to the right leads to the solitary farmstead of Aiats at the foot of the towering Cingles where the descent will later end. Continue straight on, however, following the signs for »Santuari de Cabrera«. The narrow track leads up the valley and near the stream, narrows again and then becomes a trail. Always following the blue markings, ascend in bends through the pretty beech wood, climbing to a stretch of open woodland with a trail junction. A fairly level trail

Startlingly steep cliffs rise from the plains.

continues to the left but follow the blue markings to the right to climb further. When the trail levels out, reach the crest of the ridge.

The path now leads in a south-easterly direction along the ridge of the Cingles. Pass through open woodland at first, then along the softly rolling, grassy slopes of the **Pla d'Aiats**, 1285m, sporting solitary juniper bushes. Pass by the tumbledown remains of the Cortals del Pla d'Aiats (to the right of the trail and nestled in a hollow of the slope, the buildings are the starting point for the return route!) and with these behind, reach the southern peak of the Cingles with an upright sign »L'Esquirol 2003«. The level platform with a thrilling, sheer edge is a nice place to take a break and enjoy a splendid view.

Take the same trail back to the Cortals (on the wall, a blue marking can be seen). Along an indistinct trace through the grass, descend the slope and head toward a large beech tree to begin the climb down. A step-like trail at first, the route leads along the foot of a rock face and, past that, descends quickly, often along steep, stepped slabs of rock. Climbing down through the wood, reach the pasture slopes of Aiats and end at a stately solitary oak surrounded by box tree scrub. Skirt around to the right of the farmstead and follow the track to reach the junction at the start of the walk. Here, turn left to return to the **Pont de la Rotllada**.

6 Circular walk around the Salt de Sallent near Rupit

A pretty little village with a magnificent landscape

Rupit – Salt de Sallent – Pujolràs – Rupit

Starting point: Car park at the village limits of Rupit, 840m.
Walking times: Rupit – Salt de Sallent 1¼ hrs, Salt de Sallent – Pujolràs ½ hr, Pujolràs – Rupit 1¼ hrs; total time 3 hrs.
Ascent: About 200m.
Grade: Easy circular walk.
Trail markings: Trail signs; a smattering of yellow markings.
Refreshment: None en route; Rupit.
Map: El Collsacabra, 1:25,000 (Editorial Piolet).
Info: Information centre in Rupit; ✆ 938.522083.

The Salt de Sallent near Rupit.

Notice: During periods of overflow at the Salt de Sallent, take the trail to the left; this leads upstream for a stretch and reaches a safe place to cross over large yellow-marked boulders. On the other side, after a few metres, meet up with a forest trail which leads to the right and back to the waterfall.
Tip: The wide ranging plateaux of the Cingles from Rupit and Tavertet provide first-rate terrain for mountain bikers. Brochures are available in the information centre in Rupit. Mountain bikes can also be hired there.

Even by itself, the village of Rupit with its picturesque houses and narrow streets is worth a visit – many tourists include in their itinerary a short excursion here with a circular tour of the town. Most of them neglect, however, to take a ramble in the fantastic surroundings of the Cingles. The vertical, sheer cliffs form an awesome amphitheatre sliced through by the spectacular Salt de Sallent. The walk leads from Rupit up to the heights of the Cingles and passes the delightful waterfall.

From the car park in **Rupit**, cross the bridge over the Riera de Rupit. Continue 20m along the street, then turn left and over the suspension bridge (sign »Pont Penjat«) to cross back again over the stream into the old town centre. Turn right onto the little main street, passing the church and the adjacent house with the wooden verandas. Here turn immediately left into the passageway and, at a wooden signpost for »Senders del Salt de Sallent« to the left, is the return point for the route. Continue straight ahead, however, along the cobblestone trail down to the stream and then cross over the bridge to the other side. Here turn left to continue along the stream. Shortly afterwards, arrive at a point near the splendid waterfall Salt del Molí Rodó, cross over a tributary stream and meet up with the tarmac road to Sant Joan de Fàbregues. Turn left onto this and continue, enjoying superb views of the Cingles. Reach a junction past a small house: the right fork is »Sant Joan de Fàbregues« but turn left to the next junction. Here turn left again onto the chained-off dirt road. The road makes a long bend turning back again and then runs along the edge of the vertical cliffs where the **Salt de Sallent** (730m) crashes down in a sheer drop. Shortly before, a signed junction has been passed: to the left, a direct return to Rupit is possible. Instead, turn right onto the trail towards »Pujolràs« and cross over the stream (→ Notice!) and past this, the road immediately ascends again. Soon after, reach a sign for the nearby »Mirador del Salt de Sallent« which is built directly above the cliff's edge – a good place to take a break in the shade of trees with an excellent view of the waterfall.

Now continue along the road that soon levels out and skirts the Cingles de Pujolràs – towering on the other side are the sheer cliffs of the Baga de les Baumes with the craggy monolith of L'Agullola. Past a road forking off to the left (signposts) and shortly before the gorge of the Torrent del Gravet, reach the pleasant meadowland of **Pujolràs**, 820m; a colossal rock lies to the left of the trail. A footpath leads to the right down to the stream that immediately disappears into the narrow gorge. There are abseil anchors attached to a tree on the left bank for canyonists to use to descend into the gorge.

Go back to the Salt de Sallent and, just before reaching it, turn right onto the forestry trail. This ends at a spring in the cliff face; here, turn right onto the trail to continue, passing by the Salt del Molí Rodó (a path to the left leads down to the waterfall). After crossing a little tributary stream, the trail ascends over steps traversing a rock face and then leads along terraces below the houses of **Rupit** and past a tunnelled-through house, reaching the spot on the cobblestone trail that was passed at the beginning of the walk.

7   Roc de Frausa, 1443m

On the border between Albera and Garrotxa

Car park – Santuario de les Salines – Coll del Pou – Roc de Frausa and back

Starting point: The car park on the main road between La Vajol and Coll de Manrella, 604m. From Agullana, drive along the GI-501 to La Vajol; now take the turn towards the Coll de Manrella until reaching a restaurant on the left-hand side of the road; a little further and also to the left is a signed track – park here.
Walking times: Car park – Les Salines 1¾ hrs, Les Salines – Coll del Pou ¾ hrs, Coll del Pou – Roc de Frausa ¾ hr, return 2½ hrs; total time 5¾ hrs.
Ascent: About 900m.
Grade: Technically easy but quite a long walk with great differences in height.
Trail markings: Sometimes yellow trail markings. From the Coll del Pou to the Roc de Frausa without a distinct path, but nevertheless easy to follow.

Refreshment: None en route; La Vajol.
Map: Céret (IGN 2449 OT); Institut Géographique National, 1:25,000.
Info: Oficina de Turisme in La Vajol; ☏ 972.535101.
Notice: The return route can be shortened somewhat. On the Coll del Pou at the sign »Refugí de les Salines«, take the path on the right. This merges with the track near a concrete conduit for a steam between the cliff face chapel and the Santuario.
Alternative: **Pic de les Salines**, 1333m. At the ridge, follow the ridgeline path to the right. This ascends at first to the left of a rocky outcrop then climbs up to the ridgeline and continues to Pic des Salines. Total time there and back: ¾ hr.
Tip: Visit the pretty little village of La Vajol.

The first destination for this walk is the secluded Santuario de les Salines – the name comes from the many abandoned salt mines in the area. Afterwards, continue along the panoramic ridgeline border to the Roc de Frausa; here you can enjoy exquisite, unobstructed views.

At the **car park**, trail signs point to the destination for the first stretch. Follow the ascending track through the wood, at first passing the »Font del Cucut« to the right of the trail and later a stone house. Here reach a fork; bear left to continue through a mixed forest, sometimes catching a glimpse of the reservoir of Boadella. After a long stretch of almost constantly ascending trail, meet up with a track coming from Macanet de Cabrenys. Turn right here (after a few metres ignore a tarmac road forking left and signed »Collada dels Pous / Roc de Frausa«) and follow the sign for »Santuario de les Salines«. Along the forestry trail through slopes of beech and pine, first reach the little chapel of Mare del Déu, built into the cliff. Past this and a few minutes later arrive at the strikingly-constructed **Santuario de les Salines**, 1070m, part of which has been turned into a *refugi*.

From the grand forecourt of the building, the signed path to »Pic de les Salines« heads north. Marked with yellow blazes, this climbs up the slope through beech scrub to reach the ridge. The path to the right leads to Pic de les Salines (→ Alternative), but turn left to continue along the broad ridge between juniper, pine and boulders. The path skirts around to the left of the little group of crags Roc del Pou, and past these descends to the **Coll del Pou**, 1250m.

To the left of the saddle, the tarmac road passes nearby and another road meets up with it to the right. The white/red marked GR 10 forks off left from this in a few metres and heads into the beech wood. Do not follow the GR, but instead ascend from the saddle straight ahead in a westerly direction through the splendid slope of beech trees. The open wood is easy to cross without orientation problems. Reach an open hilly dome where a transmitter installation comes into view. A path, at first rather indistinct, follows the ridge and continues toward the installation. Once there, keep to the right to pass it and continue along the boulder-strewn ridgeline to reach the **Roc de Frausa**, 1443m.

The Santuario de les Salines and the mountain of the same name.

Albera Natural Park

The contrast could hardly be more dramatic: here, the winding coastal road near Portbou, crammed between the sea and the rising mountain chains of the Pyrenees – and barely 30 km westward, the streamlined transit via highway and motorway over the Coll del Pertús. Not a bottleneck at all, rather a wide passage through the eastern Pyrenees, the pass has enjoyed a strategic status since days long past, made evident by the Fort de Bellegarde. From an elevated vantage point (Walk 8) the mighty fortress exudes its former significance in controlling this mountain pass. It is said that Hannibal crossed here in his march on Italy and, thousands of years before that, the pass served as corridor for the early settlement of the Alt Empordà, evidenced by the fascinating, wide-spread relics of Megalithic culture – dolmens (stone tombs) and menhirs (standing stones). The economically important axis between Roussillon and Catalonia is also the quickest way to the Costa Brava for many holidaymakers – albeit at the cost of missing out on the Albera Mountains and their foothills with olive groves, vineyards and oak forests.

The information centre for the »Paratge Natural d'Interès Nacional de l'Albera« is located in Espolla, with a lovely old town quarter. The protected zone embraces a mountainous landscape with distinctly different features: in the western half are dense and diverse woodlands, whereas the seaboard is characteristic Mediterranean terrain with a predominate garrigue scrub. The Albera Mountains, formed from metamorphic rock, reach their highest point at Puig Neulós, 1257m (Walk 10), along the main ridge at about 1000m – not exactly commanding, but high enough for a superb view of the Cap de Creus and of nearby France. On the other end of the main ridge, 500m lower and quite near the coast, the Querroig (Walk 15) marks the final stone bastion with fantastic views of the wave-ravaged rocky coast and the inlets and bays between Banyuls-sur-Mer and Llança.

Different tracts of the Alberas have been designated a natural park since 1986 (total area: 3428 hectares), divided into the greater zone around the Requesens castle between Pic de Llobregat and Pla de les Eres and the significantly smaller zone around the Monestir de Sant Quirze de Colera, between Puig de la Calma and Coll del Teixo. Two tiny nature reserves are additional.

The mountains here are moderately high and and the passes are fairly easy to cross, encouraging early and extensive settlement of the southern foothills. The rich cultural heritage confronts the walker at every bend and sometimes even seems to follow in his tracks, for example during the dolmen circular route (Walk 11), an attractive combination of cultural sites and natural scenery. Numerous finds from the Megalithic culture reaching back to the Neolithic period (4th – 2nd millennia BC), make the area a veritable treasure chest.

Vineyards in the foothills of the Albera Mountains.

The Romanesque Benedictine cloister of Sant Quirze de Colera is perched on a plain where a number of streams converge, flowing from their sources and down the surrounding mountain slopes. The venerable complex still offers much to see and, due to a picturesque setting, the cloister attracts many visitors; strike out on foot or just picnic in the shade near the spring. Starting here, walks can be made in every direction; the most popular is the ascent to the Coll de Teixo and along the ridge to the Coll de Banyuls (Walk 13). Long tours can be undertaken over the high ranges of the Alberas, always following the border of Spain and France. The quintessential ridgeline tour can be found in the middle region of the Alberas, between Pic de Sallfor and Puig dels Quatre Termes (Walk 12).

In the western region of the natural park, yet another monumental construction stands as a pivotal point: the renowned Requesens castle, recently restored and open for viewing at the weekend. Just across from here lies the deeply revered chapel of Santa Maria de Requesens, in a romantic setting and presenting a delightful view of the countryside – and a little restaurant for the walker who would like to enjoy a culinary break. The marvellous forests and idyllic spots near the castle and the chapel inspire short excursions, passing ancient kilns for producing lime and bricks, »ice caves« and mountain springs (Walk 9).

8 Puig dels Falguers, 750m

Only a »foothill« of the Alberas but with an excellent panoramic view

La Jonquera – Santa Llúcia – Puig dels Falguers and back

Starting point: La Jonquera; car park on the Plaça Nova, 110m. The car park is located at the southern village limits next to the Plaça del Ayuntamiento (city hall).
Walking times: La Jonquera – Santa Llúcia 1¼ hrs, Santa Llúcia – Puig dels Falguers 1¼ hrs, return 2 hrs; total time 4½ hrs.
Ascent: 640m.
Grade: Long walk with strenuous ascents.
Trail markings: GR-11 (white/red); also yellow trail markings.
Refreshment: None en route; La Jonquera.
Map: Paratge Natural d'Interès Nacional de l'Albera (Mapa topogràfic), 1:25,000 (ICC).
Info: Information centre for the natural park in La Jonquera; ℂ 972.554.354.
Tip: Fort de Bellegarde near El Pertús is worth a visit.

The Puig dels Falguers is not a very striking elevation and only of medium height, but this mountain in the extreme western end of the Albera chain offers an extraordinary view; on clear days, the view takes in the Canigou and the broad plain of the Baix Empordà all the way to the Golf de Roses. The delightful walk through scenic landscapes is complemented half-way through by the 12th/13th-century church of Santa Llúcia. Here one can find shady picnic places near mountain springs and barbecues set up to provide a lovely spot for a pleasant sojourn.

In **La Jonquera**, start from the car park and pass through the archway to the nearby Plaça del Ayuntamiento on the Carrer Major (the information centre is to the right and down the street). Continue through the smaller archway and along the Carrer Sant Miquel. Follow this to the Plaça de la Muralla then turn right onto the Carrer Cantallops until the end, where a signpost points to »Santa Llúcia«. Take the ascending forestry road and then bear left at a fork. The road narrows now and becomes rutted while ascending steeply for a long stretch. Finally, meet up with another forestry road that immediately forks: following the wooden sign for »Santa Llúcia« continue straight on, and after a few metres fork off left along a path (faded white/red markings and a yellow arrow) providing a short-cut to merge once again with the forestry road. Follow this to the right, then cross over an old track and in a left-hand bend take another short-cut forking off to the right (trail markings on stone). Meet up again with the forestry road then continue straight ahead until reaching a right-hand bend where an indistinct narrow path – marked by cairns at the trail head – forks off left. After a couple of paces, trail markings reappear. The path meets up with the forestry road again; follow this now to the left and the little church can already be seen through the trees. As soon as the road begins a slight descent, take a path to the left marked by cairns. When you come to a fork, once again bear left to reach the enclosed spring »Font de Santa Llúcia«. From here bear right, climbing up the pretty terraces and passing the natural, bubbling spring, to finally reach the **Església de Santa Llúcia**, 430m.

Near the roofed barbecue place, the route continues to the left with a prompt ascent through the densely overgrown slopes, and soon a clear view opens up of Canigou to the west and Coll del Pertús with its imposing fort. At a signed junction, continue straight ahead in the direction of »Requesens« (the path to the left leads to Castell de Rocaberti). At the following fork, bear right to continue along the more distinct trail (cairns) until reaching a conspicuous upright boulder sporting a large white-red cross. Here a footpath forks off right to stacks of boulders; in an ascent with stretches of scrambling, finally reach the **Puig dels Falguers**, 750m.

Mediterranean ambience on the way to Puig dels Falguers.

9 Circling Requesens

Excursion in the surroundings of the famous castle

L'Anyet bridge – Requesens – Castell de Requesens – L'Anyet bridge

Starting point: Bridge over the Anyet stream, 400m. In Cantallops, follow the signs for »Requesens«. At the town limits, it is generally an easy drive along a dirt road for 5.2 km until reaching the bridge; park here. Straight on, the bumpy road ascends in sharp bends to Requesens; turn right and cross the stream. Immediately afterwards, turn left, and after 1.5 km arrive at the Castell de Requesens.

Walking times: Total time 2¼ hrs.

Ascent: About 240m.

Grade: Easy circular walk along forestry tracks and walking paths; strenuous ascent to Requesens.

Trail markings: Different coloured markings; part of the route is the GR-11 (white/red).

Refreshment: Requesens; Cantallops.

Map: Paratge Natural d'Interès Nacional de l'Albera (Mapa topogràfic), 1:25,000 (ICC).

Info: The information centre for the natural park is in Espolla; ℂ 972.545079.

Tip: A tour of the Castell de Requesens is worth while. Opening hours at the weekend and on holidays from 11 am – 6 pm.

The castle fortress of Requesens, built on a wooded summit, once served as a far-reaching watch post over the surrounding countryside. Painstakingly renovated at the end of the 19th century, today the castle is a pivotal point for excursions into the densely wooded surroundings. The hamlet of Requesens, situated nearby and harbouring the renowned Mare de Déu chapel, presents an idyllic counterpoise to the grandiose construction. Both attractions will be included in this easy circular walk and, along the way, several other more subtle sights are also included in the programme.

The chapel at Requesens.

Right at the beginning of the walk, the most difficult stretch must be confronted: the ascent to Requesens. Starting at the car park at the **Anyet bridge**, go back about 50m and leave the road behind by turning right along the white/yellow-marked path. This ascends through the wooded slope to a track; turn left here to reach **Reque-**

sens, 500m, and its chapel. Turn back again and follow the white/red-marked GR-11 for a while. Along the track and past the path used in the ascent, pass the Font Rovellada de Dalt located on the left-hand side; to the right are the ruins of an old sawmill. The track crosses a stream and then turns down the valley. Ignore the forestry road signed »Puig Neulós« approaching from the left and, after a few more paces, turn left onto the forestry road blocked off by a chain. Right at the start and to the left lies the walled-in Forn de Rajols, an old brickwork kiln. Descend along the track to the stream and cross the wooden bridge to the other side. At the junction immediately after, continue to the right and reach the Torrent de Coll Pregon. Heading upstream, a yellow-marked path ascends after a few minutes to the Pou de Glaç: the wall-enclosed »ice cave« is well-preserved and is worth the short detour. Go back again and cross the stream over rocks. 100m further on, meet a fork to the right that leads to a weir with rare swamp cypresses – a cosy little place to take a break! Go back and continue the tour along the track and reach a large dry stone wall enclosing pastureland. Here is yet another chance for a short excursion: the GR turning off to the left leads to a restored limekiln adjacent to which the Refugí Barraca del Forn de Calc (no warden) has been built. Return to the corner of the dry stone wall and take the forest path signed »Castell 300 m«. This ascends to the **Castell de Requesens**, 500m. Once there, the wide access road to the left of the round tower leads to the castle entrance. Shortly before the entrance, descend along steps on the left-hand side to the track below, cross over this diagonally and pick up a yellow-marked path that provides a short-cut and returns to the track near the ruins of Mas Corral Nou. Follow this for a few paces and before the track begins a right-hand bend, turn off left again (yellow markings on a stone). At the beginning, the path is extremely indistinct and descends in a few minutes to the tumbledown farmstead Can Picardia. Once there, continue diagonally left and slightly downwards to the Santa Maria de Requesens chapel (Esglesia Vella) with its restored apse. Now turn right along the track – in the bend immediately following, the energetic walker can take up yet another excursion at the sign »Dolmen 800 m« – and back to the **bridge** spanning the **Anyet**.

10 Puig Neulós, 1257m

To the Alberas' highest mountain

Castell de Requesens – Coll Pregon – Puig Neulós – Roc dels Tres Termes – Castell de Requesens

Starting point: Castell de Requesens, 500m. In Cantallops, follow the signs for »Requesens« along the dirt road, which is easy to drive, for about 5.2 km to reach the bridge spanning the Anyet stream. Drive over the bridge and at the fork following immediately after (sign »Castell«) bear left along the ascending road to continue about 1.5 km to reach the castle. Parking possible in front of the castle driveway.

Walking times: Castell de Requesens – Coll Pregon 1¾ hrs, Coll Pregon – Puig Neulós ¾ hr, Puig Neulós – Roc dels Tres Termes ½ hr, Roc dels Tres Termes –

Castell de Requesens 2½ hrs; total time 5½ hrs.

Ascent: 757m.

Grade: A long but not difficult walk along tracks and trails.

Trail markings: Sparse yellow markings; a stretch of the GR-11 (white/red) along the return route.

Refreshment: None en route; Cantallops.

Map: Paratge Natural d'Interès Nacional de l'Albera (Mapa topogràfic), 1:25,000 (ICC).

Info: The information centre for the natural park is in Espolla; ✆ 972.545079.

Tip: Pay a visit to Requesens with the Mare de Déu chapel (→ Walk 9).

The mighty fortress at Requesens is the starting point for the walk.

FRANCE

Puig Neulós
1257

Coll del Pou

Refugi de
la Tanyareda

oc dels
es Termes

Coll Pregon
1005

Roc de les
Cabres

ESPAÑA

Roc del
Colom

Font
ovellada

equesens

GR 11

Castell
de Requesens
500

P

tallops

0   1 km

The mighty fortress of Requesens in the western natural park of the Serra de Albera is the starting point for the »push to the peak« of the Puig de Neulós. This benign mountain is the highest point of the sensational ridge and offers an open view in every direction. The prettiest eye-catcher is the Canigou Massif toward the west, often blanketed with snow well into early summer and strikingly contrasted with the green forests of the Albera.

At the **Castell de Requesens**, take the trail forking off from the last bend before the fortress. This is signed »Refugí« and leads through an oak forest descending to an open pine wood with a trail junction. Diagonally from the left, the GR-11 meets the forestry road and then turns off right along the tall dry stone wall. Cross over the GR-11 and take the broad forestry road diagonally right. At an easy rate of ascent, walk through an oak forest with a few solitary cork oaks; higher up, this gives way to beech trees.

Without leaving the main trail, reach a major road junction: the fork sharp right leads after ten minutes to a marvellous meadow slope near the Roc del Colom – a beautiful panoramic spot to take a break. The circular route, however, continues straight ahead; the track soon narrows and ascends quickly to the ridge, finally ending up at the **Coll Pregon**, 1005m, near a sign for the natural park.

Here, turn left and follow the distinct path that leads along the ridgeline and through lovely terrain with spreading beech trees. The views on both sides are excellent; the Puig de Neulós towers in front and sports an immense telecommunications mast. Continue on and to the right of the trail lies the Refugí de la Tanyareda (CAF self-catering mountain hut for 8–10 persons). Afterward, reach the enclosed spring of the same name. At first, the path heads straight for the »summit«, then turns diagonally right and winds in a very steep ascent up to the fenced-in aerial installation on the **Puig Neulós**, 1257m.

View sweeping to the French Canigou.

Changing direction towards the southwest, follow the ridgeline, keeping to the left of the pasture fence and descending easily, reach the Coll del Pou at a gate. On the »French side«, a tarmac road passes by; to the left, a track forks off along which the return route will be made later on. At first, however, continue further along the ridgeline to the nearby rocky hillock of the **Roc dels Tres Termes**, 1128m, where a lovely viewing point awaits.

Back at the gate, take the track that descends in wide bends and leads through a pleasant beech wood. Keeping to the main trail, pass by the striking Roc de les Cabres, a towering greenish rocky crag situated to the right of the trail. Now two bridges follow, crossing tributary streams. Once again, enter an oak forest and finally, at a barrier and the sign »Puig Neulós«, meet up with the forestry road coming from Requesens. Follow this to the left, then immediately turn left onto the track blocked by a chain. From here, follow the route described in Walk 9 to return to the **Castell de Requesens**.

The summit marking on the Puig Neulós can hardly be overlooked.

11 The dolmens and menhirs from La Jonquera

Natural scenery and cultural history for idlers

Circling the Estanys de la Jonquera

Starting point: The road to Capmany at km 2,4 on the GI-601 from La Jonquera to Cantallops. Signs on the right-hand side of the road: »Conjunt megalític dels Estanys«.
Walking times: Total time 2 hrs.
Ascent: Hardly any ascent.
Grade: Easy circular ramble.
Trail markings: Yellow.
Refreshment: None en route; Cantallops,

La Jonquera.
Map: Paratge Natural d'Interès Nacional de l'Albera (Mapa topogràfic), 1:25,000 (ICC).
Info: The information centre for the natural park in Espolla; ✆ 972.545079.
Tip: The picturesque hamlet of Peralada near the N-260 is worth an excursion. The extensive castle grounds make for an interesting visit.

An excursion into the megalithic culture: dolmen, menhirs and burial sites present stone relics from the earlier settlements of the region, against the backdrop of the Albera mountain chain and the agrarian countryside, as well as Mediterranean woods and little marsh lakes. The area is a protected nature reserve.

Walking along the wide **road**, follow the sign »Conjunt megalític dels Estanys« until reaching a junction near a little marsh lake to the right of the track. The track to the left leads to the driveway for the farmstead **Mas Baleta**, around which are grouped three dolmens bearing the same name. To visit the first, turn left in front of the driveway and soon arrive at the dolmen vestiges, not far from a small hill. Turn back again and follow an indistinct path (watch for yellow markings on stone!) at the edge of fields to the

Dolmen de Mas Baleta II with its roof plate missing. From here, the path leads on to a small ditch that is crossed a metal footbridge. Directly after, bear left for a short excursion to the scant remains of the Dolmen de Mas Baleta III.

Turn back now and stay on the footpath until meeting a track; turn right onto this and pass through a reforested area of pine to reach a stone-built refugí on a road. Here, bear left for 50m, then at the sign »Menhir del Querafumat« turn off to the right. An old, marked forestry road leads from here in a few minutes to

a signed path. Here, turn left and pass through lovely Mediterranean flora to reach the Menhir dels Estanys II, then continue on to the nearby Menhir dels Estanys I. Afterwards, the path meets up again with the old track walked before. Follow this to the left and soon arrive at the Dolmen dels Estanys II on the right-hand side of the trail. The beautifully reconstructed tomb, built with local granite, dates from around 3,000 BC. The signed path turning off left at the dolmen leads directly to the Dolmen dels Estanys I on an intersecting road. Here, turn left to reach a track. Take this to the right for a short stretch then meet a wide track with the sign »Mas Baleta«. Turn left onto this and continue straight on to return to the starting point.

Menhir del Estanys: stone relic of early settlements.

12 Along the ridge between Pic de Sallfor, 980m, and Puig dels Quatre Termes, 1156m

Gripping scenic contrast on every side

Coll de Banyuls – Coll del Pal – Puig dels Quatre Termes – Pic de Sallfor – Coll de Banyuls

Starting point: Coll de Banyuls, 357m. Nearest village Espolla, 110m. Starting at Espolla, the ridge on the border can be easily reached via a 10 km long, mostly tarmac-paved road. Signposts in the village.

Walking times: Coll de Banyuls – Coll del Pal 2½ hrs, Coll del Pal – Puig dels Quatre Termes 1¼ hrs, Puig dels Quatre Termes – Pic de Sallfor 1¼ hrs, Pic de Sallfor – Coll de Banyuls 1¾ hrs; total time 6¾ hrs.

Ascent: About 930m.

Grade: Very long hike with great differences in height and some very steep ascents.

Trail markings: Yellow trail markings; GR 10 (white/red).

Refreshment: None en route; Espolla.

Map: Paratge Natural d'Interès Nacional de l'Albera (Mapa topogràfic), 1:25,000 (ICC).

Info: The information centre for the natural park in Espolla; ✆ 972.545079.

Notice: Self-catering mountain hut at the Coll de Banyuls (room for about 14 persons).

Tip: The circular drive from Coll de Banyuls along a tarmac road to Banyuls-sur-Mer and then return along the coastal road N-260 via Portbou and Llançà.

Both summits lie on the main ridge of the Pyrenees in the middle of the Serra de l'Albera. The climb to Pic de Sallfor is a hiking experience on its own; the continued walk along the spectacular ridge crossing to Puig dels Quatre Termes, with high pastureland, natural rock gardens and copses of trees, is the epitome of walking pleasure. Opening up incredible views over the French Côte Vermeille and the Costa Brava coastline, it is certainly the Alberas' most sensational tour!

Begin at the **Coll de Banyuls** and head in a north-westerly direction, ascending steeply along the ridge of the Puig de les Eres. After a more level stretch in between, the trail steepens once again, climbs over the smaller Puig de les Eres and then continues through a pretty holm oak wood ascending to a junction. The trail climbs straight ahead to the Pic de Sallfor, but take a little detour by turning right and following the sign for »El Rimbau«. Keeping at about the same height, the yellow-marked trail makes a wide bend along the eastern slopes of the Pic de Sallfor.

Heading for the Puig del Quatre Termes.

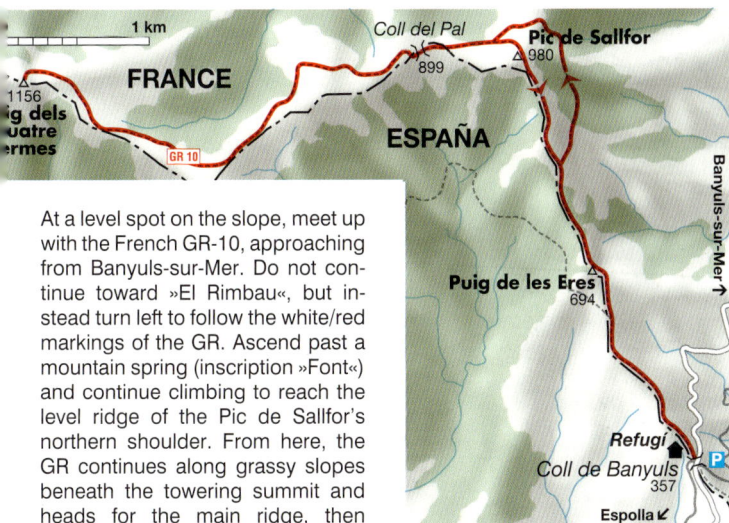

At a level spot on the slope, meet up with the French GR-10, approaching from Banyuls-sur-Mer. Do not continue toward »El Rimbau«, but instead turn left to follow the white/red markings of the GR. Ascend past a mountain spring (inscription »Font«) and continue climbing to reach the level ridge of the Pic de Sallfor's northern shoulder. From here, the GR continues along grassy slopes beneath the towering summit and heads for the main ridge, then reaches the **Coll del Pal**, 899m. The striking crag lying ahead – Roc de Santa Eulàlia – can be skirted around to the right along the grassy northern slopes of the ridge without much change in height. Now pass a small saddle, and skirt around the Puig de les Guades along its northern slopes. Perched on the summit is a clearly visible stone tower. The trail now heads toward the Coll de la Maçana, in front of which a mountain spring is situated; pass the saddle and then climb along the eastern slopes of the Puig dels Quatre Termes towards its pleasant north ridge. Ignore the trail forking off to the right towards Couloumates, instead turn left onto the ridgeline and ascend to **Puig dels Quatre Termes**, 1156m, with a marked summit.

Return along the same trail to Coll del Pal. Past the saddle, leave the GR behind by bearing right and then continue (without a distinct path) through the rugged and exposed western slopes towards the Pic de Sallfor. The summit, composed of tilted, layered plates of rock, is easy to make out. After a stretch of easy scrambling, reach the summit of the **Pic de Sallfor**, 980m. Now follow the yellow markings, skirting left around the neighbouring secondary peak. The trail then drops steeply downwards, at the same time keeping mostly to the course of the ridge, and along longer stretches near a fence that safeguards the pastureland from the sheer edge. At the signpost »El Rimbau«, meet up again with the approach trail and return along this to **Coll de Banyuls**.

13 Circular walk in the eastern Albera Natural Park

Mountain and valley walk around the cloister of Sant Quirze de Colera

Sant Quirze de Colera – Coll del Torn – Coll de Banyuls – Coll de la Plaja – Sant Quirze de Colera

Sant Quirze de Colera.

Starting point: Car park near the restaurant »Corall de Sant Quirze«, 180m. From Vilamansicle, along the signposted dirt road to Sant Quirze de Colera.

Walking times: Sant Quirze – Coll del Torn 2¼ hrs, Coll del Torn – Coll de Banyuls 1½ hrs, Coll de Banyuls – Coll de la Plaja 1¼ hrs, Coll de la Plaja – Sant Quirze ¾ hr; total time 5¾ hrs.

Ascent: About 700m.

Grade: Long hike with stretches of steep ascent.

Trail markings: Yellow trail markings; the last third of the route along the GR-11 (white/red).

Refreshment: None en route; there is a bar/restaurant near Sant Quirze; Vilamaniscle.

Map: Paratge Natural d'Interès Nacional de l'Albera (Mapa topogràfic), 1:25,000 (ICC).

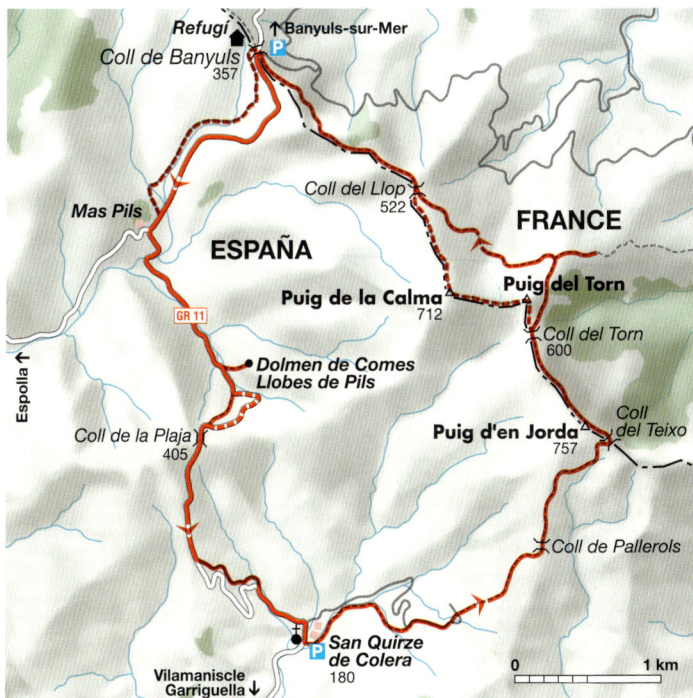

Map labels:
- Refugi
- Banyuls-sur-Mer
- Coll de Banyuls 357
- Coll del Llop 522
- Mas Pils
- ESPAÑA
- FRANCE
- Puig de la Calma 712
- Puig del Torn
- Coll del Torn 600
- GR 11
- Espolla
- Dolmen de Comes Llobes de Pils
- Coll de la Plaja 405
- Puig d'en Jorda 757
- Coll del Teixo
- Coll de Pallerols
- San Quirze de Colera 180
- Vilamaniscle Garriguella
- 0   1 km

Info: The information centre for the natural park is in Espolla; ✆ 972.545079.
Notice: Self-catering mountain hut on the Coll de Banyuls (room for about 14 persons).
Alternative: Puig de la Calma, 712m. On the Coll de Torn, continue left and, past the »Paratge Natural« sign, take a footpath ascending the ridgeline to the Puig de la Calma. From here, continue along the ridgeline to descend to the Coll del Llop.
Tip: Sant Quirze de Colera. The Romanesque Benedictine cloister, one of the most significant monuments in this region, boasts the basilica, remains of the cloister courtyard, housekeeping buildings and fortifications – some parts are under restoration.

The Romanesque cloister Sant Quirze de Colera is situated in a broad valley basin where the waters of numerous mountain streams collect. In summer, the lovely surroundings are popular with visitors. The circular walk along the ridge between the Coll del Teixo and the Coll de Banyuls shows the many differing features of this section of the Serra de l'Albera nature reserve, and offers sweeping views to as far away as the Canigou Massif.

Spring near St. Quirze.

Starting at the **car park**, head left past the cloister and descend to the stream; cross over the wooden bridge and over the stepped trail to the cosy little spot at the spring. The trail leads past the spring and forks at the same time. Bear left, following the signs for »Coll de Pallerols« and ascend through Mediterranean undergrowth until reaching another signpost. Here the trail levels out and heads northwards for a while through the slopes below the rugged ridge. Now a very pronounced ascent follows to the Coll de Pallerols.

Here, turn left towards »Coll de Banyuls« and continue along the delightful ridgeline trail above the valley of the Torrent de la Balmeta, while enjoying a view of the Canigou region. At the following fork, remain on the trail ascending left and shortly afterwards turn off right to a shepherd's shelter built of natural rock; here the trail turns again to the left. After a sometimes easy, sometimes steeper ascent, reach the Coll del Teixo. Here, follow the ridge by turning left, at first to the slightly higher Puig d'en Jorda and then in a leisurely descent to the signposted **Coll del Torn**, 600m.

From the pass, it is possible to cross over via the Puig de la Calma (→ Alternative); however remain on the yellow-marked trail and skirt around to the right of the Puig del Torn until meeting an obvious fork. Bear left here and cross over the northern slopes of the Puig de la Calma. Sometimes descending, sometime levelling out again, the hiking trail cuts through numerous stream beds and then, on the signposted Coll del Llop, 522m, merges with the trail approaching from the Puig de la Calma. In a rapid descent, the trail now follows the ridgeline again, and continues along an old track. Skirt around to the right of the Puig de les Forques summit and, past this, reach the **Coll de Banyuls**, 357m.

From here, either follow the tarmac road left or take the trail starting at the pass. This leads below the road, traversing the slope, and then follows the stream bed until coming to a meadow; continue left to meet the road again. This immediately becomes a dirt road. Near the formidable farmstead Mas Pils, change over to the road forking left in the direction »St. Quirze«. Starting here, follow the GR-11. On the way, there is an opportunity to make a fifteen-minute excursion to the well-preserved Dolmen de Comes Llobes de Pils.

Shortly after this, in a sharp left-hand bend in the road, a signed trail makes a short cut to the right. This ascends steeply, leads past an enclosed mountain spring and finally climbs back up to the dirt road. Turn right to continue and shortly afterwards reach the **Coll de la Plaja**, 405m. Remain on the dirt road, passing by a little path leading to the Font dels Cossos, and soon after take the yellow-marked short cut forking off to the left that rapidly descends to **Sant Quirze de Colera**.

Dolmen de Comes Llobes de Pils.

14 Puig d'Esquers, 606m

Sea and mountain views from Llança's »native mountain«

Coll de la Serra – Sant Silvestre – Puig d'Esquers – San Martí de Vallmala – Coll de la Serra

Starting point: Coll de la Serra, 250m. From Vilamaniscle's village limits, follow the signs to the Casa de Colónis Tramuntana, where the street becomes a dirt road. From this point, it is 1.6 km until reaching the road junction on the Coll de la Serra.

Walking times: Coll de la Serra – Sant Silvestre ¾ hr, Sant Silvestre – Puig d'Esquers 2¼ hrs, Puig d'Esquers – Sant Martí de Vallmala ¾ hr, Sant Martí de Vallmala – Coll de la Serra 1½ hrs; total

The little chapel of Sant Silvestre.

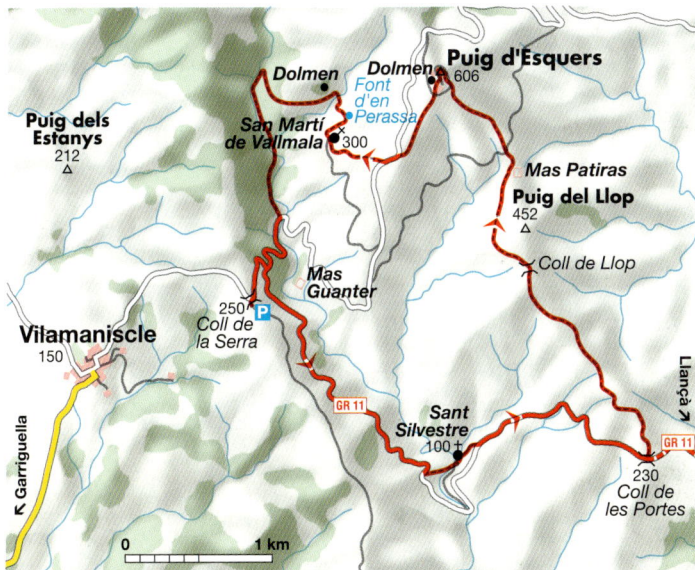

time 5¼ hrs.

Ascent: About 500m including ascents followed by compensating descents.

Grade: Long and demanding hike with very steep stretches of ascent and descent.

Trail markings: Local walking trail with yellow trail markings; a stretch of the GR-11 (white/red).

Refreshment: None en route; Vilamaniscle.

Map: Paratge Natural d'Interès Nacional de l'Albera (Mapa topogràfic), 1:25,000 (ICC).

Info: Information centre for the natural park is in Espolla; ℭ 972.545079. Information is also available at the Oficina de Turisme in Llançà, Avenida Europa, 37; ℭ 972.380855.

Alternative: The walk can also start in Llança. By km 17,8 on the N-260, a road with trail signs turns off to the right. From here, follow the GR-11 towards »Sant Silvestre de la Valletta« until reaching the Coll de les Portes and meeting up there with the route described below. This adds about 1 hr to the walking time.

Tip: Llança's music festival in July is well-worth a visit. Information provided by the tourist office.

The mountain ranges in the interior near Llança offer the best outlooks for sweeping vistas over the bays of Colera all the way to Port de la Selva. The very best is the Puig d'Esquers; as the highest point in the Serra de la Balmet, the mountain also provides a privileged view over the Albera chain that stretches to the Canigou Massif. Added ingredients to this tour through the »wild« mountain region include cultural monuments, chapels and dolmens.

On the **Coll de la Serra**, take the forestry road descending left and follow this until reaching a tight, right-hand bend with a fork. Here, bear right to follow the sign for the »Ermita Sant Silvestre« and continue mostly on the same level above the valley of the Riera de Valletta. Below and to the left, the sprawling ruins of Mas Guanter can be seen. Just after an abrupt right-hand bend a building comes into view, situated on the floor of the open valley. Here, turn left away from the track along a yellow-marked side path (to the right and painted on rock, find a white/red GR blaze!). The path descends rapidly to the valley floor and to the nicely renovated little church of **Sant Silvestre**, 100m.

After crossing the valley stream, and near the apse, take the path which ascends through the terraced slopes and then meet up with a track. Turn left to reach the Coll de les Portes, 230m, where another track ascends from Llança (→ Alternative). Here, leave the GR-11 behind and follow the sign »Dolmen« by turning left onto the narrow path (yellow markings on trees). A steep ascent continues towards the Puig Tifell; however the summit will be skirted around to the left and on the level. Enjoying lovely views – the Puig d'Esquers is easy to locate as the highest peak to the north – the trail now continues along the slopes of the mountain range, ascends for a short, steep stretch towards the conical needle peak of the Puig del Llop, levels out again and continues along its western slope to Mas Patíras. Directly

The dolmen Puig d'Esquers I.

past the farmstead ruins, a marked path to the right provides a short cut; this soon meets up with an intersecting track from which a very steep, narrow trace forks off. Ascend along this and further up, the trace becomes a real path. Ignore a fork with the sign »Dolmen« and continue in the direction to »Puig d'Esquers«. After the trail bends to the left and has remained level for a while, another steep ascent begins in a straight line towards the summit. Shortly before the end, cross over a track to reach **Puig d'Esquers**, 606m, with a little house and a surveyor's marking.

Some metres below the little house, signs have been secured to a pine tree. Follow the sign for »Vallmala«, turn southwards and immediately reach the Dolmen Puig d'Esquers I.

Inland from the coast: the Valletta Valley.

From here, continue on towards a solitary pine tree at the side of the track and pick up the very faint path that descends along the expansive and bare ridge in a south-westerly direction. Yellow markings can be discerned from time to time. At a sign meaning »no through road«, meet up with a track, turn left for a few metres and then immediately turn right again onto a marked footpath blocked by a wire. This descends as straight as an arrow to the little church of **Sant Martí de Vallmala**, 300m, of which only the apse remains. Here, turn right to continue towards »Vilamaniscle«, pass a round, stone shepherd's hut and then reach the spring Font d'en Perassa, enclosed in a little hut. From here, follow a narrow and sometimes rutted path, signed »Dolmen Passatge«, that descends to a stream. Cross over and continue along the slope on the other side heading down the valley.

The route that follows is a little overgrown, however markings can still be found. Ignore a signed fork that leads to the right to a dolmen situated 30m higher, and continue through densely overgrown terrain until reaching an old grassy trail. Turn left onto this, following the Torrent de la Balmeta. Along the way, skim the edge of a planted field. Afterwards, cross over the valley stream three times and then meet a bend in a track with a sign pointing to »Vilamaniscle«. Turn right to ascend through a cork oak wood – a farmstead can be seen below in the valley – reach the fork that marks the start of the circular route and turn right to return to the **Coll de la Serra**.

15 Querroig, 672m

Where the Pyrenees sink into the sea

Coll dels Belitres – Querroig and back

Starting point: Car park on the Coll dels Belitres, 155m. From Portbou along the N-260 towards France; park about 100m before the border at a large lay-by with a white building on the left-hand side of the road.
Walking times: Coll dels Belitres – Querroig 1¾ hrs, return 1½ hrs; total time 3¼ hrs.
Ascent: 517m.
Grade: A ridge walk that is not difficult.

Trail markings: Sometimes yellow trail markings.
Refreshment: None en route; Portbou.
Map: Paratge Natural d'Interès Nacional de l'Albera (Mapa topogràfic), 1:25,000 (ICC).
Info: Oficina de Turisme in Llançà, Avenida Europa, 37; ✆ 972.380855.
Tip: Along the coast, you can visit the monument to Walter Benjamin in Portbou. The trail there is signposted.

The »peak« of Querroig stands as the last bastion of the Pyrenees before the mountain range drops rapidly and, along the promontory between Portbou and Cerbère, seems to disappear into the Mediterranean. The view of the coastal areas is just as beautiful as the one taking in the Albera Natural Park. Unfortunately, only a few scattered foundation walls from the former castle on Querroig still remain.

At the **car park**, start off along the track that passes to the right of a house and ascends. A short way past the house, this levels out and continues on through cultivated slopes. As soon as the trail levels out, however, leave this behind by turning right and ascending without a trail to the ridge of the low summit. Here, meet up with a track that ascends along the hilltop ridge. Follow the track – to the right and somewhat below, a wider road that has ascended from the other side of the border runs parallel. Through densely overgrown slopes, remain on or just a little away from the ridgeline. The track drops down to Coll del Frare (surveyor's marker 599) and, further along the ridgeline, reaches the Coll de la Farella (surveyor's marker 598) with a sign pointing to »Querroig«. Here, the track merges with the wider road, but continue along the pretty path marked with yellow blazes and leading through typical Mediterranean garrigue. To the left of the trail lies a dolmen missing a roof plate.

Querroig: summit with a sea view.

The trail continues in a steadily steep ascent, sometimes through under-brush taller than a person, then skirts around left of the craggier terrain marking the summit of Querroig and ascends to the ridgeline that stretches on the left-hand side over to the »Coll de Querroig« (sign). Remain, how-ever, to the right and after a few metres, reach the summit of **Querroig**, 672m, where you will find the ruins of a medieval castle.

»Cap de Creus« and »Aiguamolls de l'Empordà« Natural Parks

The Pyrenees do not in fact end on the coast at Portbou at all; just as if to avoid their inevitable disappearance into the Mediterranean sea, the mountains suddenly turn southwards before reaching Colera, bend once again to the east, form the Serra de Rodes and then extend far into the sea as the Cap de Creus, finally sinking into the water at the tip of the cape, the »Punta«.

Out of the flat plains east of Figueres and only a few metres above sea level, the Serra de Rodes Mountains rise up. Sant Salvador Saverdera, 670m (Walk 18) is the region's highest mountain and can be spotted from far away and from all directions due to the ruins of the castle bearing the same name that crown the peak like a summit marker. Be sure to savour the superb view from the summit as long as possible – sweeping far into the Pyrenees, over the lowland plains of the Alt Empordà, far below to Roses and its bay and all along the rugged coast – not missing the cape with the seaside town of Llançà and, especially beautiful, the white-washed El Port de la Selva on the shore of the turquoise Mediterranean sea. Hulking and almost intrusive, the Monestir de Sant Pere de Rodes (Walk 19) poses in front of this marvellous backdrop, 150 metres lower down along the mountain slopes. The former Benedictine cloister of pre-Romanesque origins appears as a huge block of stone and rightly so: an impenetrable fortification that rules over the Peninsula at the same time. The famous cloister has been thoroughly renovated and, in the high season, attracts droves of tourists driving along the road towards the pass between Vilajuïga and El Port de la Selva. The view in the opposite direction focuses on a little white church at the foot of a towering ragged peak, the Ermita Sant Onofre (Walk 17), a tranquil, cosy spot, only accessible by foot, preferably along the old trail from Palau-Saverdera. Dolmen (quite significant both in number and cultural importance) can be found in the Serra de Rodes, mostly along the western slopes of the mountains with scenic hiking paths (Walk 16) connecting the individual stone-built cultural sites.

A jagged peninsula marks the easternmost point of Spain, the major part containing the Parc Natural del Cap de Creus, established in 1988. This attraction alone is almost enough to give credit to the cape's tourist draw. «Almost», because the bleak landscape exudes its own irresistible magic, a kind of primeval natural essence probably most compellingly manifested on the Punta del Cap de Creus (Walk 22): here at Spain's »world's end«, rock, sea and light combine to produce a fascinating natural extravaganza – Mother Nature in the raw. Strangely enough, after the almost obligatory visit to the lighthouse, only a handful of holidaymakers take the last strides to the bizarrely-sculpted cape's end, torn and ravaged by water and wind. For the

The bay of El Port de la Selva.

hard-nosed walker tackling the long-distance trail GR-11 through the Pyrenees, here is the beginning – or the end, depending on the itinerary chosen. The Cap de Creus' coastline (Walks 20, 21 and 23) is made up almost entirely of inlets; a straight stretch is virtually non-existent. Everywhere, deep and wide clefts in varying dimensions cut into the cape's interior: *cala* is the word used for inlets, *badia* for bays. *Bais* are the locations chosen for the towns of Cadaqués and El Port de la Selva, two marvellously-situated seaside settlements located on the eastern and northern ends of the cape, and offering contrasting ambience. Cadaqués, chic but unobtrusive, profits from Dalí's renown while El Port de la Selva displays the congenial atmosphere of a more commonplace harbour town. Even when these towns are used as mere starting points for lovely coastal walks, both are a »must« for a Costa Brava holidaymaker. The settlements of Llança and Roses both lie along the quiet seaboard of the cape. Roses sprawls along the wide, bending bay of the same name and is, without a doubt, the tourist centre for the region (Walk 24); nonetheless, the town has managed to preserve a pleasant individuality in its heart of hearts.

South of Roses and inland from the long sandy beaches, an extensive wetland can be found, flat as a board and criss-crossed by lagoons, the remains of a mostly drained marshland, fenced-in for protection nowadays to encompass the Parc Natural dels Aiguamolls de l'Empordà (Walk 25). The area provides excellent breeding grounds and a welcome migratory stop-over for numerous species of birds and is therefore an extraordinary site for bird-watching. The proximity of the sea and the mountain-like backdrop of the Cap de Creus present a scenic kaleidoscope.

16 The dolmens of Vilajuïga

A culturally seasoned ramble through the Serra de Pau

Road to Sant Pere de Rodes – Puig Margall – road to Sant Pere de Rodes

Starting point: Car park on the road to Sant Pere de Rodes (GIP-6041), 50m. A good kilometre after Vilajuïga's village limits and near the sign for the natural park »Cap de Creus«, park at a lay-by with the sign »Dolmens«.

Walking times: Car park – Puig Margall 1¾ hrs, Puig Margall – car park 1½ hrs; total time 3¼ hrs.

Ascent: 380m.

Grade: An easy circular route overall, but some stretches of strenuous ascent; the re-

turn route requires some sense of direction.

Trail markings: Yellow trail markings.

Refreshment: None en route; Vilajuïga.

Map: Parc Natural del Cap de Creus (Mapa topogràfic), 1:25,000 (ICC).

Info: Oficina de Turisme in Llançà, Avenida Europa, 37; ℂ 972.380855.

Tip: Mas Ventós, 435m. The renovated farmstead with beautiful and spacious picnic grounds offers a first-class viewing point over a wide area of the Alt Empordà.

Numerous dolmens bedeck the Mediterranean garrigue-blanketed slopes around Vilajuïga and Pau. These bear witness to the extensive settlement of the mountainous area near the seaboard between the 4th and 2nd millennia BC. In the course of the walk, some of the most striking examples can be seen, accompanied by far-reaching views of the Albera Mountains and the plains of the Aiguamolls Natural Park.

At the **car park**, follow the sign »Dolmens« and at the same time enter the Cap de Creus Natural Park. A track leads along the side of the Barranc de la Coma de l'Infern and through once-cultivated terrain with old terraces; at the end, the track becomes a trail that forks. Bear left, cross over the stream and ascend through garrigue vegetation. Soon meet up with the Dolmen de la Vinya del Rei, the largest specimen to be found in the entire Vilajuïga region. The trail cuts back a little before ascending directly along the slope to the Dolmen de Garollar. The view to the Albera mountain ranges opens up during the approach to the Dolmen de la Taloisa and a few minutes later, after passing over large plates of rock, reach the Dolmen de les Ruïnes sporting two roof plates. Five minutes later, meet up with the Dolmen de la Carena; the trail merges into the road to Sant Pere de Rodes. Turn right to continue along this; 30m further on, pass a yellow arrow marking on the

One of the many dolmen along the circular route.

right-hand side of the road that points to the trailhead for the return route. After a total of about 300 metres, reach the Dolmen de les Vinyes Mortes. The first of the dolmen pair can be seen just off the road, the second can be reached in a few minutes along a marked detour descending the slope. Returning to the road and continuing right for only a few metres, come to a sign pointing to a yellow-marked path presenting a short cut to avoid a bend in the road. Meet up again with the road, continue directly to the other side and pick up the ascent trail to the Dolmen de Puig Margall; soon after this, reach **Puig Margall**, 430m.

Now turn back again to the spot with the yellow arrow marking and then turn off left from the road along the marked path. This immediately ascends for some minutes, then drops down again and continues, sometimes over plates of rock. In places where the route is hard to discern, keep an eye out for yellow trail markings. To clear a precipitous section of slope, the trail ascends again somewhat and then continues steadily downwards, heading towards a prominent rocky ridge. Along this, pass by the cave Cova del Llop and soon after, descend into the valley through thinly wooded slopes and return to the fork in the trail where the walk began. Turn right to return to the **car park**.

17 Sant Onofre, 394m

A delightful viewing point on the western slopes of the Muntanya de Verdera

Palau-Saverdera – Sant Onofre and back

Starting point: Palau-Saverdera on the GI-610; car park at the restaurant »Terra Nostra«. Drive straight on along the main village street to the village limits; here, follow the signed access road until reaching the restaurant.

Walking times: Palau-Saverdera – Sant Onofre 1½ hrs, return 1¼ hrs; total time 2¾ hrs.

Ascent: About 310m.

Grade: Not a difficult walk with short strenuous stretches of ascent.

Trail markings: GR 92 (white/red markings); the route also follows stretches of the local walking trails no.1 and no.8 (yellow markings).

Refreshment: None en route; Palau-Saverdera.

Map: Parc Natural del Cap de Creus (Mapa topogràfic), 1:25,000 (ICC).

Info: Oficina de Turisme in Llançà, Avenida Europa, 37; ✆ 972.380855.

Tip: The bodega on the GI-610 near Vilajuïga with local wines.

On the western slopes of the Sant Salvador Saverdera, the little white chapel of Sant Onofre is sure to catch the eye. Towered over by the jagged crags of El Fito, the chapel rests in an exposed spot on a rocky spur that offers what one could expect: a superb view sweeping from the Bay of Roses over the mountainous hinterland of Figueres and Gerona all the way to the French Canigou Massif. This pleasant spot is perfect to while away the time.

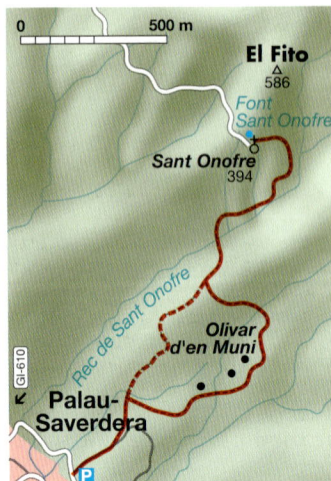

At the **restaurant** »Terra Nostra«, take the signed trail towards »Sant Onofre«. This leads through abandoned farmland that is sometimes bordered by dry stone walls. After walking along a dry stone wall as tall as a man, the trail splits into two trails at the corner of the wall; turn right here and follow the GR through overgrown terraces. On the way, pass a number of cultural monuments: first a roofless dolmen located a few metres to the left of the trail, then a wonderfully-preserved menhir on a terrace which is pointed out by a yellow arrow, then a few paces further, the Dolmen d'en Puet, reached by a path to the left. Further up, the trail bends to the left, passes a conspicuous cork

Marvellously perched upon an outcrop of stone: the Sant Onofre chapel.

oak with three trunks then a tumbledown dolmen and finally descends rapidly into a valley. At this point, the trail merges with a yellow-marked path approaching from the left. Turn right onto this, cross over the little stream bed and after a mostly level stretch of trail, meet up with a stony track flanked by walls. Turn right to continue; soon the track narrows into a path that at first follows on the level along a stream bed, the Rec de Sant Ofre, then crosses over and begins a steady ascent on the other side. Further up, reach the ancient cultivated terraces of the hermitage. The stream valley bends to the left and the trail leads onto the left slope, winding up to the chapel of **Sant Onofre**, 394m, situated beside a spring of the same name; towering high above is the striking craggy summit of El Fito.

To shorten the return route, keep on the stony track that descends steeply and then becomes a narrow trail that meets up once again with the tall dry stone wall at the first fork.

18 Sant Salvador Saverdera, 670m

An enchanting view from Cap de Creus' highest mountain

Pau – Mas Ventós – Coll del Mosquit – Sant Salvador Saverdera and back

Starting point: Pau, 30m; Plaça Major (village square).
Walking times: Pau – Mas Ventós 1½ hrs, Mas Ventós – Coll de Mosquit ½ hr, Coll de Mosquit – Sant Salvador Saverdera ¾ hr, return 2½ hrs; total time 5¼ hrs.
Ascent: 640m.
Grade: Long and demanding hike.
Trail markings: Local walking trail (yellow markings).
Refreshment: None en route; Pau.
Map: Parc Natural del Cap de Creus (Mapa topogràfic), 1:25,000 (ICC).

Info: Oficina de Turisme in Llançà, Avenida Europa, 37; ✆ 972.380855.
Alternative: Return via **Sant Pere de Rodes**, 520m. While climbing down from the castle, remain on the trail descending to the cloister. From there, take the concrete-paved road to the Santa Helena chapel where a signed trail leads over the ridge and to the forestry road.
Tip: Sant Pere de Rodes cloister. Opening hours: Oct. 1 to May 31 from 10 am – 5:30 pm; June 1 to Sept. 30 from 10 am – 8 pm. Closed on Mondays (except on holidays).

Like a monument to days gone by, the ruins of the Castell de Sant Salvador rise up from the ridge of the Verdera Mountains. Even from afar, they catch the eye and challenge the walker to a climb rewarded by the view from above: a fantastic scenic display over vast stretches of the Alt Empordà – across to the Albera Mountains and far into the Pyrenees, over the plains surrounding Figueres and into the mountainous interior, from the lovely bay

The peak vis-à-vis: ruins of the Castell de Sant Salvador.

at El Port de la Selva over to the Golf de Roses, the entire Cap de Creus and endlessly out to sea.

From the **Plaça Major** continue along the village street, following the signs for »Creu Blanca / Sant Pere de Rodes« and reach an information board with trail signs at the end of the road; the trail begins here. In a pleasant ascent, this leads along the gentle foothills of the mountain range. Wide at the beginning, the trail narrows, ascends steeply through dense garrigue and reaches a signed junction. Turn right (on the left, a sign for »Sant Pere de Roda por Mas Margall«). While crossing over old terraced slopes with pretty dry stone walls, the increase in height reveals a sample of the various landscapes there to enjoy. Shortly after, the summit topped with castle ruins also comes into view. After a couple of wide bends in the trail, reach the Creu Blanca, a limestone cross from the 15th century and a pretty spot to take a break. Continue at first along level, terraced slopes then begin an ascent and merge with a forestry trail that leads to the road from Vilajuïga to Sant Pere de Rodes (GIP 6041). Turn right and continue for about 200m, then turn right onto the forestry road blocked by a chain and reach the nearby **Mas Ventós**, 460m. The grounds around the partially renovated farmstead offer barbecue areas, picnic tables in the shade and a marvellous view: a lovely place to take another break.

Continue in an easterly direction along a track skirting around a group of wooden benches. Ignore a track signed »Sant Onofre« that turns to the right and, 50m past this, turn right onto the forestry road towards »Coll de Mosquit«. During the pleasant ascent, pass the trail that turns off to the left and heads for the chapel »Santa Helena« and the Sant Pere des Rodes cloister (→ Alternative). Continue the ascent to reach the **Coll del Mosquit**, 550m. The modest saddle presents a surprisingly spectacular view over the sea and the harbour town of El Port de la Selva. Now continue the walk along the yellow-marked path bearing just a little to the right of the Coll. This heads towards the summit dome with the castle ruins, crosses over the ridgeline and continues along the broad ascending trail that winds up from the cloister. Here, continue the climb up to the castle – a visit to the castle fortifications is a must! – pass to the left and then, along the ridge path and slightly descending at first, continue the ascent over to **Sant Salvador Saverdera**, 670m.

19 Monestir Sant Pere de Rodes, 520m

Beautiful flowers and bewitching views over the northern Cap de Creus

La Vall de Santa Creu – Sant Pere de Rodes – La Vall de Santa Creu

Starting point: La Vall de Santa Creu, 150m; car park before the village.
Walking times: La Vall de Santa Creu – Sant Pere de Rodes 2¼ hrs, Sant Pere de Rodes – La Vall de Santa Creu 1¼ hrs; total time 3½ hrs.
Ascent: 370m.
Grade: Not a difficult walk although with strenuous stretches of ascent.
Trail markings: Local walking trail no. 10 (blue and yellow); a stretch along the GR 11 (white/red).
Refreshment: None en route; a bar in La Vall de Santa Creu (only open in summer), otherwise El Port de la Selva and Llançà.
Map: Parc Natural del Cap de Creus (Mapa topogràfic), 1:25,000 (ICC).
Info: Information centre for the natural park near the cloister ✆ 972.193191.
Alternative: Ascent to the Castell de Sant Salvador de Verdera, 680m. In front of the entrance to the cloister grounds, take the trail to the right and signed »Sant Salvador«. Along steep, ascending bends, this climbs up to the castle. The trail forks in front of the castle: following the yellow trail markings to the left, reach the summit

of Sant Salvador Saverdera, 670m; the white/red trail markings to the right lead through the gate into the interior of the castle ruins. Additional time needed ¾ hr.
Tip: See Walk 18.

The hamlet of La Vall de Santa Creu in the hinterland of the coast between Llançà and El Port de la Selva is the starting point for a circular walk leading to the renowned cloister grounds of Sant Pere de Rodes. In early summer, a colourful display of flowers lines the lovely trail which passes through abandoned once-cultivated slopes and offers numerous opportunities for various views of the coast, cliffs and mountains of the northern Cap de Creus. At the car park of **La Vall de Santa Creu**, a signboard sketches out the circular walk. Take the street into the village and then follow the signs for »Sant Pere de Rodes«. Bear right at a fork as pointed out by a red arrow, towards »Corrals d'en Marcelet« (the blue-marked trail no.10 bearing left will be used for the return!) and ascend between dry stone walls through old terraced slopes. Steep at first, then in moderate ascent, pass by the corrals of Marcelet enclosed by dry stone walls to finally reach the Coll del Perer. At the saddle, meet up with the GR 11 ascending from Llança. Follow this in a bend to the left towards »Sant Pere de Rodes« and after a quite strenuous ascent meet up with a track. Turn left to continue along this and, below the ridge, skirt around the Puig de la Granja. At a tumbledown building (shortly before, pass a sign »Paradolmen de la Pallera Roca Galera«) meet up with the road connecting Vilajuïga and El Port de la Selva. After a few paces in the direction of the cloister, turn right to leave the road behind and take the wide access road to the picturesquely situated Santa Helena chapel. From there, descend to the car park and continue along the concrete-paved driveway to the **Monestir Sant Pere de Rodes**, 520m.

The return route starts in front of the cloister entrance to the left. Take a few strides towards »Informació« and then immediately turn left (trail sign) to a spring with a viewing point in the shade. From here, a grassy path leads through the slopes and soon meets up with the road to El Port de la Selva; cross over this. On the other side and at the trail sign, pick up the delightful trail leading over the slope and then descend rapidly, following yellow markings, to cross over into the main valley where the village (the starting point) is lying. Through abandoned terraced slopes enclosed by small walls and passing fields and vineyards at the end, return to **La Vall de Santa Creu** and the fork at the start of the walk.

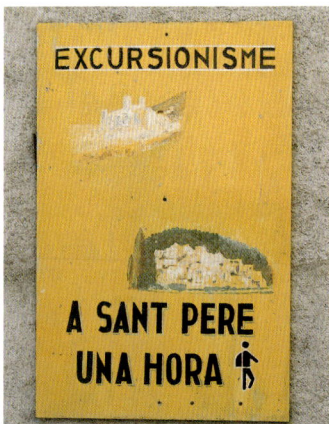

»Antique« tourist ad.

Old dry stone walls line the trail.

20 Punta Blanca

Through pristine stretches of coastline near El Port de la Selva

Cala Tamariua – Cala Fornells – Punta Blanca and back

Starting point: Car park on the Cala Tamariua, 25m. In Port de la Selva drive north along the harbour road, continue along the coast road and follow the sign »Ruta Panoràmica« until reaching the car park at the end of the road.

Walking times: Cala Tamariua – Cala Fornells 1¼ hrs, Cala Fornells – Punta Blanca ¾ hr, return 1¾ hrs; total time 3¾ hrs.

Ascent: Ca. 180m.

Grade: Experience in scrambling, sure-footedness and some sense of direction are required. Sometimes without a distinct path or even without any path at all.

Trail markings: None.

Refreshment: None en route; El Port de la Selva.

Map: Parc Natural del Cap de Creus (Mapa topogràfic), 1:25,000 (ICC).

Info: Oficina de Turisme in El Port de la Selva, Mar, 1; ✆ 972.387025.

Tip: The scenic and picturesquely situated settlement of Selva de Mar (along the GIV-6121 from Port de la Selva). 10 minutes away, the trail leading to the Font dels Lledoners also reaches the Visigoth church of Sant Sebastià – well worth a visit.

East of Port de la Selva, the rugged coast awaits us with extreme contrasts in natural scenery. Towering cliffs with rock faces battered by wind and sea,

On the Punta Blanca.

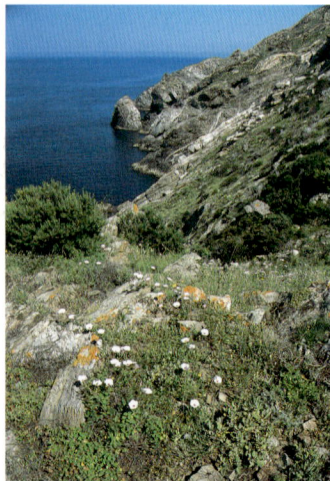

meagre vegetation, the remains of earlier attempts at cultivation and, in between, incredible inlets cut deep into the coastline: all this characterises an untamed coastline that belongs to the most pristine on the Cap de Creus. Always at the seaside, the walk leads to the Punta Blanca, the northernmost promontory of the Cap de Creus.

From the car park, take the paved trail with steps down to the **Cala Tamariua**, walk along the beach to the other side of the bay and then pick up the coastal path which is easy to see. This leads mostly on the level through slopes and crosses over to the Cala Cativa. Here cross the first gully of a brook and soon meet up with an even more deeply cut gully with a light-coloured band of rock. Cross over the stream bed and reach steep, terraced slopes with old dry stone walls, some of which are well-preserved. Now, once again cross over a gully that empties into a tiny inlet. Here is the rugged promontory of the Cap Mitjà along which numerous paths lead at various heights. These all meet up again above the steeply plunging sheer cliffs. Watch out – a short stretch passes uncomfortably close to the plummeting edge and then crosses over a rocky little valley. Now, again following a distinct path, head for the narrow and precipitous Cala Fornells – during the descent over the cramped and craggy path to the bay, choose every step and handhold carefully. Walk the gravel beach of the **Cala Fornells**, 0m, to the other side – the Rec de Fornells has made a deep cut in the rocky

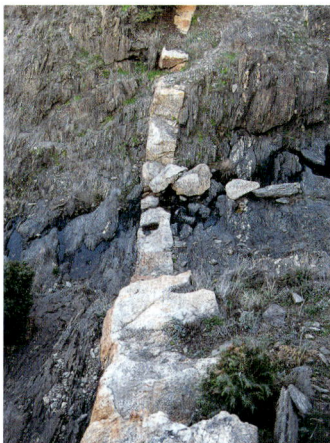

Remarkable bands of rock mark the coastal cliffs.

cliff above the bay and plunges down as a beautiful waterfall! – and scramble up at the most likely spot on the steep rugged, rocky slope for about 10 or 15m to reach a footpath that continues on at about the same height. At first, circle around the little Cala Torta, then cross over the influx into a larger bay and ascend along the left side of this. Beneath a striking overhanging rock, the path turns away to the left from the overgrown stream bed and skirts around the cliff – cairns mark the way – climbing steeply. Afterwards, the way levels out temporarily, becomes indistinct once more, then ascends again

heading toward a rugged, pointed crag; pass by this by keeping right and scrambling through a little »rock arch«. Along rugged, rocky slopes, head for the small grassy saddle to the right and next to the light-coloured, slanted, layered rock of the coastal cliffs. Once there, the **Punta Blanca** can be seen below. Taking in the view to the east and over to Cap Gros, the dome-shaped rock monolith towering out of the sea, El Boc i la Cabra, catches the eye.

21 Cala Tavallera

Along the inland route to a dreamy bay

El Port de la Selva – Sant Baldiri – Cala Tavallera and back

Starting point: The car park at the beginning of the track to the Mas Puignau, 80m. In El Port de la Selva drive north along the harbour road, continue along the coast road following the »Ruta Panoràmica« sign, then turn right onto the street with the trail sign, ascend past small villas and reach the beginning of the trail with the sign »Sant Baldiri de Taballera«.

Walking times: Car park – Sant Baldiri 1 hr, Sant Baldiri – Cala Tavallera 1 hr, return 1¾ hrs; total time 3¾ hrs.

Ascent: About 160m.
Grade: Not a difficult walk.
Trail markings: GR-11 (white/red).
Refreshment: None en route; El Port de la Selva.
Map: Parc Natural del Cap de Creus (Mapa topogràfic), 1:25,000 (ICC).
Info: Oficina de Turisme in El Port de la Selva, Mar, 1; ✆ 972.387025.
Tip: El Port de la Selva. The delightful village in a picturesque setting on the grand bay has happily secured itself against mass tourism.

Between El Port de la Selva and the lighthouse on the Cap de Creus, the prettiest part of the GR-11 is doubtlessly the first half to Cala Tavallera. Along this stretch, a surprising variety of coastal scenery is on display, although at first the vegetation appears monotonous, even desolate. Since the bay, cutting deeply into the coastline, is only accessible on foot, the walker is unlikely to meet up with any kind of »beach life« outside of the high season. At the most, a few boats may be anchored offshore.

Not much further to go: Cala Tavallera.

Starting at the **car park**, follow the track and ignore all forks. Continue on past the point where trail number 6 forks off to the right. After passing the junction for »Mas Puignau« and »Puig Gros«, soon reach another signed junction. Here, keep walking on for some minutes more along the trusty road in the direction of »Cala Tavallera«; at a sign, turn left onto a narrow trail. Pass a dog kennel, cross over a forestry road and finally reach the ruins of the hermitage of **Sant Baldiri**, 120m. Although fallen into ruin, ancient walls still convey a good impression of the original building.

Now the trail leads downwards into the idyllic little valley of the Rec de Talabre – the Mas d'en Paltré is located upstream from here – then cross over the stream and, on the other side, ascend to a signed forestry road; turn left here to continue. Near a trail sign, change over to the path forking off left that now leads over abandoned terraces. At first keeping level, then slightly descending, the trail heads straight for the wide, open bay and at the end climbs quickly down to the stony beach of **Cala Tavallera**, 0m.

22 Punta del Cap de Creus

Along the »Camí antic« to the easternmost point of the Iberian Peninsula

s'Alqueria – Punta del Cap de Creus and back

Starting point: Residencial Paratge s'Alqueria on the coast road from Cadaqués to Cap de Creus, 50m. At Cadaqués' village limits, take the road forking left to Cap de Creus (signed) and drive 2.5 km until reaching the Residencial Paratge S'Alqueria, a villa estate still under construction. At the last access road turning off to the right from the coast road (the Avinguda Paratge s'Alqueria), park just at the entrance. Here is also a sign »Camí de Ronda«.

Walking times: s'Alqueria – Punta del Cap de Creus 1¾ hrs, return 1¾ hrs; total time 3½ hrs.

Ascent: About 150m.

Grade: Sure-footedness is required for the stretch from the lighthouse to the destination point.

Trail markings: Trail signs.

Refreshment: A bar at the new lighthouse on the Cap de Creus; Cadaqués.

Map: Parc Natural del Cap de Creus (Mapa topogràfic), 1:25,000 (ICC).

Info: Oficina de Turisme in Cadaqués, Cotxe 2-A; ✆ 972.258315.

Tip: Picturesquely situated on the harbour bay, Cadaqués with its snow-white houses and narrow streets is well worth a visit. In nearby Portlligat an excursion to Salvador Dalí's house can be made. Located on the Platja Portlligat, this is now a museum and an extremely popular tourist site, so reserve early. The current opening hours are available at the tourist office in Cadaqués; or call ✆ 972.251015.

The lighthouse at the »end of the earth«.

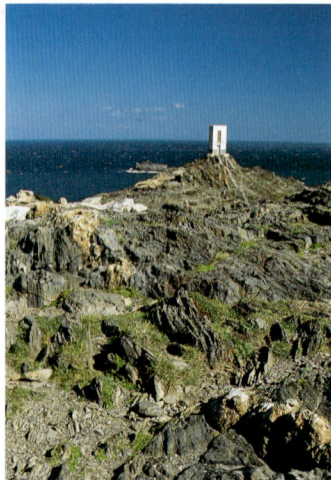

The lighthouse at the »end of the earth« marks the easternmost point of Spain. During any excursion to Cadaqués, it is almost obligatory to take a spin to the Punta del Cap de Creus – most tourists drive there and miss out on the austere beauty of the scenic seaboard and its rich variety of flora which can be enjoyed in tranquillity along the old trail between Cadaqués and the lighthouse. And having taken the time, the walker really should continue on foot to the absolute tip of the Punta del Cap de Creus, with nothing left but the open sea in front and the fantastic formations of the ravaged cliffs behind.

A few metres off the coast road and on the **Avinguda Paratge s'Alqueria**, a path turns northwards – a

0   1 km

Pic de ses Formigues 92 △

Rec de Cala Torta

Pic Palau 152 △

la Maça de Oros

84 *Far de Cap de Creus* △

Cap de Creus

Cala Jugadora

Cala Bona
Cala Torta

M e d i t e r r á n e o

Badia de Guillola

P **s'Alqueria** △51

Cap d'en Roig

Cadaqués ↓

short-cut to avoid the coast road. Descend to the height of a bay and, just past this point, the trail begins an ascent through olive groves and then merges again with the coast road. Turn right, continue for a good 100m and pass a wall-enclosed finca with olive trees. Just past the driveway, the »Camí antic« turns to the right away from the road (sign) and leads through pretty terraces of olive trees to reach a wide track. Here, turn right through a villa complex until meeting the trail sign »Guillola« where a descent begins. At this point, turn left onto the signed trail. Flanked by little walls, continue through abandoned terraces and soon cross a hillock; shortly afterwards, the lighthouse comes into view. In easy up-and-down walking, the trail leads through an ever more natural coastal area whereby the remains of earlier cultivation only accent the harshness of the terrain. Cross three small valleys, marking the water courses to the Cala Torta, Punta Prima and Cala Bona, and begin to close in on the Cala Jugadora that cuts deeply into the coastline. After crossing the watercourse flowing to the bay, the trail ascends again to the road; turn right here. In the following sharp left-hand bend, turn right onto the cobblestone GR trail (wooden posts at the side of the road). This leads to the lighthouse and the car park with information boards near which, and a little to the right (trail markings on rock), the trail continues on to descend towards the old lighthouse. Skirt around the lighthouse to the right, then descend to the final cliff tops with light-coloured horizontal layers of rock. The trail climbs around to the right and continues downwards to the »end of the earth« with the white/red GR circle on the **Punta del Cap de Creus**, 15m. This is the beginning – or the end – for the long-distance hiking trail through the Spanish Pyrenees from the Mediterranean to the Atlantic. Experienced rock-climbers could attempt scrambling down the last remaining metres of solid land until the only option left is to jump into the sea.

77

23 Around the Cap de Norfeu

Along the Camí de Ronda to a peninsular viewing point

Montjoi – Cap de Norfeu – Torre de Norfeu – Cala Jóncols and back

Starting point: Montjoi, 0m. From Roses along the coast road, follow the signs for Montjoi; car park in front of the »Ciutat de Vacances«.

Walking times: Montjoi – Cap de Norfeu 1¾ hrs, Cap de Norfeu – Torre de Norfeu ½ hr, Torre de Norfeu – Cala Jóncols 1 hr, return 1¾ hrs; total time 5 hrs.

Ascent: About 280m.

Grade: Some strenuous stretches of ascent.

Trail markings: Between Montjoi and Cala Jóncols, the GR 92 (white-red); along the excursion to the Cap de Norfeu, a distinct path.

Refreshment: Montjoi and Cala Jóncols.

Map: Parc Natural del Cap de Creus (Mapa topogràfic), 1:25,000 (ICC).

Info: Oficina de Turisme in Roses, Avinguda de Rhode; ℰ 902.103636.

Notice: To only make an excursion to the Cap de Norfeu, start off at the Cala Canadell. From Montjoi continue driving along the bumpy road until reaching the sign »Cala Canadell«; here are places to park. The route is described below; total time 1¾ hrs.

Tip: Along the way, take a swim at the lovely little sandy bay Cala Pelosa.

The Camí de Ronda between Montjoi and Cala Jóncols is a pleasant trail destined to fulfil every walker's hopes and dreams. In early summer, ramble through an ocean of flowers along the steep coastal cliffs, time and again passing delightful bays perfect for a dip in the water. For an excursion on the way, the Cap de Norfeu, a rocky promontory reaching far into the sea, almost insists on being walked. From the tip of the cape, enjoy a marvellous sweeping view southwards over the never-ending coastline.

In **Montjoi**, walk to the beach and over to the other side to pick up the rocky coastal track; follow this for 1km. At a trail sign, turn right onto the Camí de Ronda then traverse the coastal slopes, dropping down to a small bay. On the other side of the pebble beach, ascend again for a couple of metres and

then continue on the level, passing steep, rocky little inlets, descend to the Cala Pelosa, boasting a beach of fine sand. On the other end of the bay, the trail ascends again, somewhat higher, leads past a small gully (to the right is an information board – »El Pi«) and begins an arduous ascent along the steep coastal slopes. The trail is sometimes stepped. Along the ridge of the cape's promontories, the trail levels out again, changes direction and merges with the coastal track above the Cala Canadell. Now take the signed track to »Cap de Norfeu« and ignore a path to the right which climbs to the Torre de Norfeu. Just after, the track becomes a path; along this, at first pass by the walled-in cliff grotto »Cova de les Ermites« and then a path forking off which ascends to »Cova les

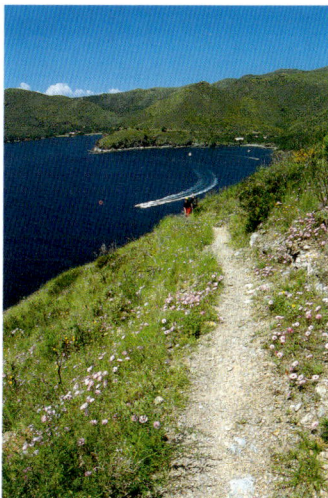

The ascent to the Cap de Norfeu.

Encantades«. High above the sea, walk through the densely overgrown slopes with a view of the cliffs on the other side. Now reach the ridge of the promontory and head for the eastern tip; at a trail junction on the way, continue straight ahead (on the return route, a turn will be made here). Pass a squat stone hut and then reach the very end of the **Cap de Norfeu**, 130m, at the edge of the steep coastal slopes.

Return to the junction last mentioned and turn left here along the leisurely ascending path through the southern slopes of the cape. Soon after, the imposant ruins of a round watchtower appears – head straight for it to reach the **Torre de Norfeu**, 160m, with an information board. Go left to pass around it and then, at the back, immediately turn right to steeply descend over rock. Now along the rapidly descending cape ridge – ignore the transecting trail that climbs down to the right and drops to a track – reach the GR trail; take this to the starting point for the excursion. At the trail sign, continue along the Camí de Ronda through the slopes above the Cala Canadell and then rapidly descend into the little valley of the watercourse that cuts to the bay. Cross the stream and immediately ascend to a small saddle, behind which the Cala Jóncols appears. Through terraced slopes, descend steeply along the trail to reach the beach of the **Cala Jóncols**, 0m.

24 Coll de Fitor, 310m

Exploring the hinterland near Roses

Pla de Can Marès – Coll de Fitor – Pla de Can Marès

Starting point: Pla de Can Marès 130m. car park near the sign »Dolmen de la Creu d'en Cobertella« on the road to Montjoi, about 1.6 km past the turn-off in Roses.
Walking times: Pla de Can Marès – Coll de Fitor 1¾ hrs, Coll de Fitor – Pla de Can Marès ¾ hr; total time 2½ hrs.
Ascent: 180m.
Grade: A fairly easy circular walk.
Trail markings: Local walking trail no.3 (orange); and yellow.
Refreshment: None en route; Roses.
Map: Parc Natural del Cap de Creus (Mapa topogràfic), 1:25,000 (ICC).
Info: Oficina de Turisme in Roses, Avinguda de Rhode; ✆ 902.103636.
Tip: Roses, on the bay with the same name. The largest settlement on the Cap de Creus can still boast a pleasant ambi-

ence with a moderate infrastructure for tourism and a number of sites worth seeing; for example, the sprawling fortifications of »La Ciutadella« with the remains of the Greek city, founded in the 8th century BC by former inhabitants of the island of Rhodes.

Along this walk, megalithic cultural sites – especially the »Dolmen de la Creu d'en Cobertella« which is striking because of its sheer size – are mixed in with a variety of scenic impressions: the bays of Roses and of Montjoi towards the south, the towering Muntanya de Verdera northwards and the surprisingly verdant hilly pastureland in the mountainous hinterland of Roses.

At the car park **Pla de Can Marès** follow the signs for »Dolmen de la Creu d'en Cobertella« while heading along the cobblestone trail to reach in a few minutes the mighty cultural site dating from the 4th to the 3rd century BC. Continue along the dry stone wall flanked trail, passing through olive groves and then the ruins of the Casa Cremada, and afterwards, the menhir of the same name as well as a burial site. Enjoying a beautiful view of the Badia de Roses, continue on through sometimes abandoned terraced terrain; the trail then slowly drops down to a brook and past that meets up with a signpost; turn right here towards »Puig Marès«. Passing some houses, the trail bumps into a road; keep right to immediately meet up with a signed junction. To the right, a quick return to the »Dolmen d'en Creu de la Cobertella« is pointed out, and to the left is our next destination, the »Cista del Llit del General«. Along the country lane and on the right-hand side, the towering »Menhir de la Casa Cremada I«, with an information board, can be seen. The pleasant valley of Mas Oliva lies to the left down below. The trail as-

View of the Badia de Roses.

cends for a while, levels out and reaches a trail junction with a narrow foot-path that drops left down to »Mas Oliva«. Continue straight ahead, however, until reaching another trail junction; here, turn left towards »Pla de Gates«. The yellow-marked path leads to a broad track on the Pla de Gates, a long, curved saddle with grassy slopes – in the past, this was one of the most important pasturelands in the southern half of the Cap de Creus. Signs draw attention to the fact that the meadows are now in the process of being turned back to nature. Turn left onto the track and reach the tiny **Coll de Fitor** (also called Coll de l'Albera), 310m, after a quarter of an hour. Also here are the ancient burial grounds of Cista del Llit del General. The view from this spot looks down upon the Montjoi Bay and further to the Cap de Norfeu, with the watchtower. Return along the track and descend to the signed trail junction; here turn left, following the sign for »Cova-Dolmen Rec de la Quarantena«. After crossing a brook, pass by the first dolmen cave at the right-hand side of the trail. Immediately after, a path forks left to the second and larger »Cova-Dolmen«. Now continue along the trail, flanked by dry stone walls, to return to the road and the **Pla de Can Marès**.

25 Parc Natural dels Aiguamolls de l'Empordà

An excursion through unique coastal marshland

El Cortalet – Bassa del Matà and back

Starting point: El Cortalet (information centre for the natural park), 2m. From the GIV 6216, take the signed turn-off to the car park at El Cortalet.
Walking times: El Cortalet – Bassa del Matà 1 hr, return 1 hr; total time 2 hrs.
Ascent: Almost null.
Grade: Easy walk.
Trail markings: GR-92 (white/red).
Refreshment: None en route; Castelló d'Empuries and Sant Pere Pescador.
Map: Parc Natural del Cap de Creus (Mapa topogràfic), 1:25,000 (ICC).
Info: The information centre for the natural park is in El Cortalet (see Notice).
Alternative: Grand circuit of the natural park. This extensive hike presents the Aiguamolls from various viewing points, although not during the breeding season when a section of the beach is closed (April 1 to June 15). On the Bassa del Matà, walk along the beach – the Platja de Can Comes – northwards and follow wooden posts marking the protected zone. Pass a row of posts running to the sea, then reach another row with a wooden hide at the limits of the natural park. (Here, the walk can be shortened along the Camí de Can Comes that heads landwards from the beach and then meets a track; here, turn left to return to El Cortalet. This indistinct path, however, may be flooded and impassable. For a current report on conditions, check at the visitor's centre before beginning the walk). Continuing along the beach, pass the Camping La Laguna and head for the mouth of the Muga; once there, turn left along the dyke between the river and the campsite until almost reaching the footbridge crossing over the Muga. Shortly before the bridge, turn left to descend to the road and then along the

track passing by Empuriabrava's sewage purification plant (»Depuradora«) following signs for »Estany Europa« and »El Cortalet«. The trail is now blue-marked and soon, past the marshy lake with two hides, turns left and passes the Can Comes. Later, the trail turns right, passes by a tumbledown house and returns to El Cortalet. The complete circuit takes 4½ – 5 hrs.

In the Mediterranean wetlands between the mouth of the Muga and Fluvià rivers, numerous species of birds nest and migratory birds make a stop off. The well-planned natural park is a model of its kind and a Mecca for ornithologists, but it is also hugely interesting for the amateur birdwatcher in regards to the feathered inhabitants of this important coastal wetland – wonderful to observe from the roofed hides along the trail.

In front of the **information centre**, a wide trail signed »Itinerari de la Massona« heads off to the right. At the beginning, this leads along the west side of the Estany de Cortalet, passes storks' nests and then continues parallel to a water channel, the Rec Corredor. Numerous observation posts or hides (»Observatoris« and »Aguaits«) are situated along the way with signs pointing them out. Past the large »Observatori Pallejà« to the left of the trail and on the Lagune La Massona, the trail makes a hook to the right and reaches the Estanys del Matà. Before taking a turn to the left, the opportunity is there to make an excursion to »Mas del Matà« and the viewing platform »Senillosa«, from which the walker can get a good overall view. Now the trail leads through an extensive wetland terrain where horses are grazing. Shortly before the campsite Náutic Almatà, turn left to cross over a small ditch and continue parallel to the track running alongside the campsite and heading directly towards the seashore. At a lifeguard's tower, reach the **Bassa del Matà** and the end of the walk.

An inhabitant of the Aiguamolls.

Baix Empordà

Marvellous rocky coves with crystal-clear water, broad beaches of fine sand, dramatic cliffs – the coastline between L'Escala and Tossa de Mar is one of the most diverse of the Costa Brava. Add the interior to the picture, and the Baix Empordà becomes a unique scenic potpourri, beginning inland from the bustling harbour town of L'Escala; a high plateau there, 150m in height, plunges back to sea level just short of L'Estartit. The expansive limestone promontory is riddled with lovely coves enclosed by rugged cliffs. Only accessible on foot and starting off at the quiet and secluded Massís de Montgrí, climb down and then back up again (Walk 27). A couple of kilometres inland, the Castell de Montgrí (Walk 26) is enthroned above the town of Torroella. The fortress castle with a sweeping view missing nothing (enjoyed to the full from the ramparts) has been built upon a garrigue-covered limestone rise bordered to the east by a tract of dunes – »Les Dunes«. Past l'Estartit, a long, level beach follows the coast; inland, an intensively cultivated farmland plain is divided by the Ter River. Then suddenly, with medieval Pals in the foreground (the centre of rice cultivation in the region) the land heaves upward to become the Massís de Begur, a mountainous seaboard promontory where the settlement bearing the same name is perched. Along the densely urbanised seaside slopes, a delightful »Mirador« can be found as well as secluded spots, pristine stretches of coast, and lush, wooded valleys (Walk 28). La Bisbal d'Empordà is the region's capital and a centre for handmade ceramics. Southwards, the granite mountains of the Gavarres rise up – however to give a more exact description, the mountain ranges are so densely-covered by holm and cork oak forests that naked rock is seldom seen. A verdant terrain, where tranquillity contrasts with the hurly-burly of the seacoast and adds relish to the walking trails found here (Walk 31). At the edge of the Gavarres toward Calonge, the wooded slopes give way to farmland; here the »lifeblood of the Costa Brava« is cultivated – wine. The first bearers were the Greeks, arriving at Empúries on the Costa Brava in the 6th century BC; only a few centuries later, the Empordà was renowned for its viniculture. A truly noble »fruit of the vine« is not likely to be found in the little wine-growing estates of the region, but solid, natural table wines are abundant; there are several opportunities for tasting during the walk to Puig Cargol (Walk 30).

Castell de Montgrí.

From Palafrugell, on the eastern edge of the Gavarres and three kilometres from the seashore, a road quite like a motorway shoots off toward the sea. This is very odd, since high-rise tourist traps, which one would expect, are not to be found here; instead, the pretty settlement of Llafranc is clustered on one of the Costa Brava's most picturesque bays. Between here and the Badia de Tamariu further to the north, the coast once again shows its wild side, untamed and unsettled, with a fantastic bay as gateway to an enchanting gorge (Walk 29).

Platja d'Aro: endless sandy beach right out of a picture postcard, backed by the usual tourist shopping street. Connected to this is the »Camí de Ronda«, contrariwise following an ancient clandestine trail for smugglers. Well-fortified and unspoilt by development, the trail leads along the coastal cliffs

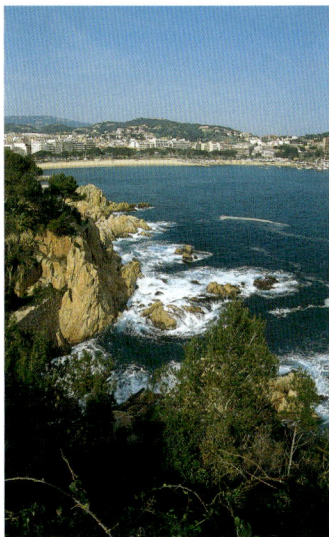

The bay of Sant Feliu de Guíxols.

crimped up on the seaboard, passing tiny coves and idyllic beaches until returning to the urban sprawl at the ancient defensive tower Torre Valentina (Walk 34).

A rocky spur at the Cala de Vigatà near Sant Feliu de Guíxols, and the Ermita de Sant Elm (Walk 34) higher up, offer the best views of the coast, stretching as far away as Tossa de Mar and towered over by the 500m higher Puig de ses Cadiretes (Walk 35). Here, the Costa Brava truly lives up to its name, with sheer cliffs dropping off into the sea and little inlets inaccessible by land. The Serra de Montclar, 400m higher, is only a hop landwards. The granite mountains are an offshoot and do not quite seem to fit in the Ardenya main ridge. To enjoy a superb 360°-view from the peak, a number of trails can be taken, as well as a recommendable route for the mountain biker ending at the Coll de Montclar (the last metres must be walked). Without a doubt, however, the most beautiful and stimulating walk is the one via the Carcaixells d'en Cama: through delightful forests and along steep, rugged cliffs where an ingenious trail, supplied with chains for safety and for handholds, leads at the end over a beguiling suspension footbridge (Walk 33).

26 Castell de Montgrí, 302m

Karst, garrigue and an imposing castle

Torroella de Montgrí – Castell de Montgrí – Les Dunes – Santa Caterina – Torroella de Montgrí

Starting point: Col-legi St. Miquel in Torroella de Montgrí, 25m. In Toroella, follow the signs for »Castell de Montgrí« that lead to a school complex with plenty of parking available. Park here and then descend a couple of metres along the street in front of the Collegi in a westerly direction to meet up with the trail sign for the Castell.

Walking times: Torroella de Montgrì – Castell de Montgrí 1 hr, Castell de Montgrí – Les Dunes ¾ hr, Les Dunes – Santa Caterina ½ hr, Santa Caterina – Torroella de Montgrí ¾ hr; total time 3 hrs.

Ascent: About 380m.

Grade: Not a difficult walk although sure-footedness is required for some strenuous stretches of ascent.

Trail markings: The GR-92 (white/red) and a local walking trail (white/green).

Refreshment: There is a bar near Santa Caterina (open at the weekend in summer); Torroella de Montgrí.

Map: Baix Empordà-Nord (Mapes topogràfics), 1:30,000 (Editorial Piolet).

Information: Oficina de Turisme in l'Estartit; Passeig Marítim, 47; ✆ 972.75 1910.

Tip: The Museu d'Arqueologia from

Empúries north of l'Escala is worth visiting. The archaeological excavations on the seaboard have uncovered Greek and Roman settlement sites from the Costa Brava's ancient past. These are split over two levels in a lovely setting and are being painstakingly restored; the presentations are most informative. Opening hours: October 1 to May 31, 10 am – 6 pm daily; June 1 to September 30, 10 am – 8 pm daily. Information is available in the museum on the premises; ✆ 972.770208.

In the flat plains of the Empordà, the Castell de Montgrí is an eye-catching feature seen from far and wide. The other way about, the view from the round towers of this medieval stronghold castle bolster the impression that the surrounding countryside was kept well under control from here. The walk to and around the limestone hillock where the castle is enthroned is very attractive, due to lovely garrigue vegetation with a surprisingly diverse spectrum of flora, and also to the novelty of the dune landscape formed by sand blown from the beaches of the Golf de Roses.

Follow the GR that begins at the **trail sign** as a country lane. This narrows after a while into a trail that is sometimes reinforced. Pass several pilgrim's

Visible from afar: Castell de Montgrí.

chapels and ascend in bends to Coll de la Creu, 199m. On the little saddle sporting a stone platform and a cross, the return route meets up here again later. Now continue to the right along the stony trail in pleasantly ascending bends to the **Castell de Montgrí**, 302m. The castle fortifications are nicely renovated and always open to the public; a tour along the castle walls with a panoramic view is a must. At the eastern side of the castle walls, a wooden signpost points to the continuation of the GR. Descend rapidly along a narrow trail through dense garrigue to reach the Coll d'en Garrigars, 215m. Now head along the level limestone ridge – en route, to the left and below, the white Santa Caterina church can be seen in the valley – to reach a white observation hut where the trail drops even steeper. Now watch out: at a path that continues straight ahead to a little saddle (Coll de Puig Roig) the proper trail makes a pronounced hook to the right and then passes through a pine wood to Coll de les Sorres and **Les Dunes**, 135m. Here, an information board explains the curious dune landscape situated in the middle of a mountainous karst area. Leave the GR behind and now follow the white/green-marked trail towards »Santa Caterina«, i.e. continue on along the forestry road and in the right-hand bend that follows, and then turn left onto the narrower forestry road. At a field, this narrows even more and begins a strenuous ascent over the Coll de Puig Roig; here, the castle comes back into view. Immediately descending again, reach the valley floor and the church of **Santa Caterina**, 140m. On the west side of the church, pick up the trail again at a trail sign. In a pleasant ascent, reach the »Coll de la Creu« and then return to **Torroella de Montgrí**.

27 Along the coast of the Massís del Montgrí

Up and down walking featuring limestone plateaux and dreamy inlets

Alt de la Pedrosa – Cala Ferriol – Cala Pedrosa – Alt de la Pedrosa

Starting point: Alt de la Pedrosa, 135m. At l'Estartit's village limits and the first roundabout, take the turn-off to »Camping l'Estartit«; follow signs for the campsite and after passing it, continue along the road to ascend to a high plain with a wide tarmac road and a number of trail signs. Park here.

Walking times: Alt de la Pedrosa – Cala Ferriol 1¼ hrs, Cala Ferriol – Cala Pedrosa

1 hr, Cala Pedrosa – Alt de la Pedrosa ¾ hr; total time 3 hrs.

Ascent: About 300m.

Grade: Not a complicated walk, but with strenuous ascents and descents to the inlets.

Trail markings: The GR-92 (white/red); stretches of the route to the Cala Ferriol are without markings; local walking trail (white/green).

Refreshment: None en route; l'Estartit.

Map: Baix Empordà-Nord (Mapes topogràfics), 1:30,000 (Editorial Piolet).

Information: Oficina de Turisme in l'Estartit; Passeig Marítim, 47; ✆ 972.75 1910.

Tip: A visit to the Medes Islands Nature Reserve. The small group of islands close to l'Estartit offers an incredible variety of underwater flora and fauna and thus counts as one of the most interesting diving and snorkelling areas in the Mediterranean. Glass-bottom boats offering easy underwater observation start off from l'Estartit. On the largest island of Meda Gran, a short walk can be made from the docking area to the lighthouse (though not during nesting season!). Information is available in the tourist office.

Between l'Escala and l'Estartit, the Costa Brava has kept much of its rugged character. The steep coastline, devoid of development, and the high plain of the Montgrí Massif are sanctuaries for the walker seeking tranquillity. Starting off from the luxuriant vegetation of limestone heights, the route descends to two of the most beautiful bays found on this steep coast, with clear waters very enticing for a dip in the sea.

On the **Alt de la Pedrosa**, follow the tarmac road at first towards »l'Escala«. Ignore the first two forestry trails turning right but at the next one (again signed »l'Escala«), turn right. After 100m, reach more trail signs and the junction for the GR-92. Keep in the direction marked »l'Escala«, i.e. turn right onto an old forestry road leading to yet another signed junction. Following signs for »Punta Ventosa« and »l'Escala«, continue left along a rocky but verdant forestry road. Enjoying a lovely view, walk across the limestone plain and meet up with a signed junction where signs to the right point out »Cala Ferriol« and »Cala Pedrosa«. At first, however, remain on the GR, heading straight on until the trail slightly widens (about 100m before reaching a trail sign that is easy to see). Here, leave the GR behind by turning right along the distinct trail pointed out by a white/red cross. The rocky path is now unmarked but the course of the trail is always clear. This descends in a straight line along the garrigue slopes and enters a wood before reaching the **Cala Ferriol**, 0m. From here, near a forest fire warning sign on the right-hand side in the wooded slope (sea view), pick up the white/green-marked trail. The trail immediately begins a steep ascent. Soon leave the wood and climb up to the limestone summit. Now continue on the rocky track to reach trail signs, turn left and descend again along a narrow footpath.

On this stretch, enjoy delightful views to the north of the Roca Foradada, riddled with holes and extending far into the sea. The path rapidly leads to the marvellous **Cala Pedrosa**, 0m. Skirting around pebbled beach landwards, head through a fine valley then ascend more steeply again to finally return to the limestone summit and a track. Turn right here and go back to **Alt de la Pedrosa**.

The undermined Roca Foradada.

28 Excursion in the Massís de Begur

Scenic contrast and sweeping views of the Costa Brava

Mas d'en Pinc – Mirador de la Creu – Cala d'Aiguafreda – es Quinze – Mas d'en Pinc

Starting point: Mas d'en Pinc, 200m. Driving from Pals, go round Begur to the left along the bypass road and then turn left at the sign for »Centre d'Estudis del Mar«. At the next street (Passeig Carmen Amaya) turn right until reaching trail signs near the Mas d'en Pinc with a high defensive tower. Park on the roadside.

Walking times: Mas d'en Pinc – Mirador de la Creu ¾ hr, Mirador de la Creu – Cala d'Aiguafreda ¾ hr, Cala d'Aiguafreda – Mas d'en Pinc ¾ hr; total time 2¼ hrs.

Ascent: About 230m.

Grade: Easy circular walk; strenuous ascents along the return route.

Trail markings: Local walking trail (white/green).

Refreshment: None en route; Begur.

Map: Baix Empordà-Nord (Mapes topogràfics), 1:30,000 (Editorial Piolet).

Information: Oficina de Turisme in Begur, Avenida Onze de Setembre, 5; ✆ 972.624520.

Alternative: Reserva Marina de ses Negres, 0m. A section of the aquatic nature reserve between the bays of Riera and Aiguafreda can be walked along an official coastal track. Turn left at the road junction and continue for a good kilometre until reaching a junction marked with a trail sign. Turn right here and keep going to the end of the road nearby. At the following trail sign, descend over steps to the reinforced trail that leads along the steep coastline. Take this to the end and then turn left along steps climbing up to a road; here, follow the trail sign »Aiguafreda« by turning left. Continue on to the last road junction and return to the starting point. This stretch is white/green marked. Total walking time about 1 hr.

Tip: Pay a visit to Pals on the C-31. The hamlet, with its renovated and embellished old town, is located in the flatlands of the interior and is the centre for the local cultivation of rice. In the spring, culinary events are organised, offering a selection of regional dishes. Information: Oficina de Turisme in Pals; Plaça Major; ✆ 972.667857.

The region around Begur is not exactly an undeveloped coastal haven. Nevertheless, a certain charm has remained which is underscored by oases of quiet, natural scenery such as the almost pristine oak forest of Quinze and some unspoiled stretches of coastline. Along the route from Mas d'en Pic, where the centre for the protection and exploration of the seacoast is currently located in Begur, lies the Mirador de la Creu, an outlook that provides a view stretching as far away as the Cap de Creus.

At the trail signs near the **Mas d'en Pinc**, head towards the »Mirador de la Creu«, descending along the road and following the »Camí de les Pedreres«. The road ends here; continue along the ascending forestry road. At a complicated junction, take the old track running diagonally right that leads into the wood and becomes a footpath. At the following fork, turn right and away from the road, continuing straight on and descending. Now the path levels out and follows a dry stone wall. After a short but steep ascent, reach a little tarmac road. This leads to the right to the foot of a stony spur where the **Mirador de la Creu**, 182m, is situated. On the viewing platform, a panoramic chart points out the surrounding features. Now turn back and stay on the winding road until reaching a complicated junction with trail signs. To the left, the trail continues to the »Reserva Marina« (→ Alternative), but turn right towards »Aiguafreda« until reaching an intersecting road; turn left (sign »Cap sa Sal«). The road leads past a car park. At the end of the car park, the trail turns off to the right. Descend along stone steps to a fortified cliff trail that leads to **Cala d'Aiguafreda**, 0m. You could take a walk around this lovely bay, but instead keep to the right of a canal inflow and reach the inn »Sa Rascassa« at the end of a road. Take this road for about 500m to a fork and continue straight ahead here, following the sign for »es Quinze«. At the sharp left-hand bend following immediately after, turn right onto the tarmac road (Carrer Garbi). Leave this again 50m on, by following the trail sign and turning left. The ascending trail soon leads through a wood and then – watch out! – suddenly hooks to the left and continues through the dense oak forest of **es Quinze** along the Riera d'Aiguafreda. At information boards, reach a nature trail which is only a part of the continued route; keep following the coloured markings and then meet up with an old well, a charcoal-maker's pit and a variety of plants and trees all with explanatory signs; finally reach the round tower of the **Mas d'en Pinc**. Here, bear diagonally right to return to the starting point.

Along the Camí de Ronda (Alternative).

29 Between Llafranc and Tamariu

One of the most beautiful coastal areas of the Costa Brava

Llafranc – Tamariu – Cala Pedrosa – Sant Sebastià – Llafranc

Starting point: Llafranc, 0m; the Plaça Major at the beach.

Walking times: Llafranc – Tamariu 1½ hrs, Tamariu – Cala Pedrosa ¾ hr, Cala Pedrosa – Llafranc 1¼ hrs; total time 3½ hrs.

Ascent: 310m.

Grade: Not a difficult walk, however some stretches along cliffs and some strenuous ascents.

Trail markings: The PR-C-107 (white/yellow) and the GR-92 (white/red).

Refreshment: Llafranc and Tamariu; Cala Pedrosa (only in summer) and Sant Sebastià.

Map: Baix Empordà-Sud (Mapes topogràfics), 1:30,000 (Editorial Piolet).

Information: Oficina de Turisme Llafranc, C. Roger de Llúria; ℭ 972.305008

Tip: The Jardí botanic de Cap Roig is worth seeing. The botanical garden south of Calella de Palafrugell houses a great variety of typically Mediterranean flora. The Costa Brava's internationally renowned jazz festival also takes place here in July and August. Information: Paratge Cap Roig, 17210 Calella de Palafrugell; ℭ 972.614582.

In the 1950's and 60's, Llafranc and Tamariu were still insider tips – little fishing villages on idyllic inlets where film stars and famous painters celebrated and partied. Now transformed into popular and renowned seaside tourist spots, during the low season the villages still maintain much of their old ambience. The circular route between the two villages leads at first through the countryside inland and then follows a rugged coastal route with a pause on the fascinating and lovely Cala Pedrosa.

Starting at the **Plaça Major** in Llafranc, turn right onto the seaside promenade and reach some trail signs, one pointing out the first destination, »Tamariu«. Walk past the nearby Oficina de Turisme while ascending the Carrer de Mossen Rafael Durán (sign »Església«) and then turn left at the street crossing, passing a white apartment complex. Now continue on the dirt road – along this stretch, a short excursion can be made by turning left and following the signs for »Dolmen de Can Mina dels Torrents«. At the signed junction, continue in the direction of »Tamariu«. The track leads through fields and then meets up with the main road (GIV-6542); turn right and 100m further on, turn left once again at a trail sign onto a forestry road. This leads through pine woods and a residential area. At a hydrant situated on the left-hand side, leave the forestry road by turning sharp right. Just after a left-hand bend, meet up with a chain-blocked path; turn right and a few metres later, turn left onto a narrow footpath. After crossing the stream bed of a little valley, the footpath ends at some villas on the main road. Here, turn right and descend to **Tamariu**, 0m. At the beach, turn right following the signs for »Sant Sebastià« and »Cala

Not a good place for a swim – steep and rugged inlet along the trail.

Pedrosa«; take the white/red-marked GR along the coastline cliffs via a sometimes unfortified trail. Keep an eye out for the markings along the short stretch over bare rock! The trail then climbs rapidly up the coastal slope, skirts around a deep gorge and then leads into pine woods. With steep cliffs towering in the foreground, continue for a short way along a forestry road, then along a forest path; finally a narrow, winding stretch protected by railings descends to the **Cala Pedrosa**, 0m. At the little beach house, take the trail heading inland and quickly ascend along the gorge with vegetation so lush, a tropical forest springs to mind. Now meet up with a signed track. Turn left here. At the following left turn, continue straight ahead and soon follow a narrow footpath through pine woods. Now climb steps to a trail sign; turn left towards »Sant Sebastià« and soon reach the summit of **Sant Sebastià**, 178m, and the ruins of an ancient Iberian settlement (»poblat ibèric«) as well as a former hermitage and a mighty watchtower. The coastline view is stupendous. At the restaurant forecourt, pick up the trail once again to reach a road with a viewing platform, taking in the Badia of Llafranc. Now descend along the coast road. Not far from Llafranc proper take the stone steps to the left, to make a short cut for a stretch of the road. They quickly climb down to the little harbour of Llafranc, on the eastern end of the bay. From here, take the street fronting the beach to return to **Plaça Major**.

30 Puig Cargol, 356m

Vineyards and woodland near Calonge

Mas Molla – Puig Cargol – Mas Molla

Starting point: Mas Molla at the north-easternmost limits of Calonge, 30m. Approaching from Palamós along the GI-660, drive through the village and past a bridge on the left-hand side spanning the river, then meet up with a Nissan garage on the right-hand side. At the very next street, turn right and ascend straight ahead until reaching an intersecting street at the end. Turn right here then take the first left onto the Carrer d'en Molla until reaching the farmstead.

Walking times: Mas Molla – Puig Cargol 2 hrs, Puig Cargol – Mas Molla 1¾ hrs; total time 3¾ hrs.

Ascent: 326m.

Grade: Strenuous stretches of ascent.

Trail markings: Local walking trail (white/green); a stretch along the way is unmarked.

Refreshment: None en route; Calonge.

Map: Baix Empordà-Sud (Mapes topogràfics), 1:30,000 (Editorial Piolet).

Information: Oficina de Turisme Calonge ℡ 972.661714

Tip: Visit one of the bodegas around Calonge and perhaps stumble upon a fine local wine.

The fertile plain surrounding Calonge is extensively utilised for viniculture. Most of the region's vineyards are concentrated here and one can see that these are cared for with painstaking diligence. The end result is a sound table wine that has not yet been commercially exploited. At first, ramble along the densely wooded foothills of the Gavarres and then get acquainted with the vine-laurelled environs of Calonge.

Pass to the left of the **Mas Molla** and at the signpost, head in the direction of »Puig Cargol«. The country lane leads to the nearby »Torre Lloreta«, dating from the 13th – 14th century and built as a defensive tower against pirate attacks. Shortly after, meet up with a little tarmac road. Turn right onto this and then at a left-hand hook, continue straight ahead onto the forestry road forking off. Climbing up and down through pine and oak woods, meet up with a

An artistically-built field hut.

broad forestry road ascending from the left and turn right onto this. In a steady and sometimes steep ascent, cross over a forestry road and then reach a junction on a small saddle where the trail markings become a little unclear. Turn right here onto the now narrow path to continue, cross a small hilltop and after a stretch of walking up and down, reach an open area near the Mas Ribot de Fitor to meet up with the PR-C-105 that leads to the »Castell de Vila-Romà«. Continue, however, towards the »Puig Cargol« by turning right onto the wide, ascending forestry road and soon reach the large column (triangulation point) perched upon the **Puig Cargol**, 356m.

To enjoy an open view, you have to get up the courage to climb the column (iron rungs). Now follow the broad, unmarked forestry road – pass a covered water reservoir with a hut – and ignore all forks. When meeting up again with the white/green-marked trail, turn right onto the clearly narrower forestry road. This meets up with another track close to the Mas Barraca; turn right onto this and continue to the Mas Ribot with three striking cypress trees.

Here, turn right onto the intersecting country lane to continue and then left at the next fork, following the sign for »Clos d'Agon«. At a vineyard with an ornate little hut, the track forks; bear right and at the fork immediately after bear left again, crossing over a stream gully. At a sign pointing right towards »Cerler Mas Gil«, turn left to continue along the track. Passing the Mas Bou, meet up with the trail sign from the beginning of the circular route and thus return again to **Mas Molla**.

31 The ancient springs near Romanyà de la Selva

An excursion in the southern Gavarres

Romanyà de la Selva – Font de Can Llac and back

Starting point: The village limits of Romanyà de la Selva, 320m.
Walking times: Romanyà – Font de Can Llac 1¼ hrs, return 1 hr; total time 2¼ hrs.
Ascent: About 100m.
Grade: Some short but strenuous ascents.
Trail markings: The GR-92-1 (white/red).
Map: Baix Empordà-Sud (Mapes topogràfics), 1:30,000 (Editorial Piolet).
Information: Oficina de Turisme Santa Cristina d'Aro; Pl. Mossèn Baldiri i Reixac; ✆ 972.837010.
Refreshment: None en route; Romanyà de la Selva.
Alternative: Another return route is possible. From the Font de Can Llac, remain on the wide forestry road and pass by the GR trail. At first climbing up and then down – with a view to the south over the mountainous interior – pass Can Poncet and return to the main road, directly at the short-cut path from the beginning of the tour.
Tip: In the immediate vicinity of Romanyà de la Selva, you can visit two other springs without much effort. The Font d'en Guitó is not far from the village: from the village limits, descend about 100m along the main road, then turn left onto a footpath to reach the pretty spring in a few minutes. The Font de la Castanyeda is a somewhat longer walk; the PR-C-110 (white/yellow) runs past the spring. Cross through the village, heading south-east and then, after about 400m, turn left onto a forestry road. Not quite 1km further on, a path to the right leads to the spring.

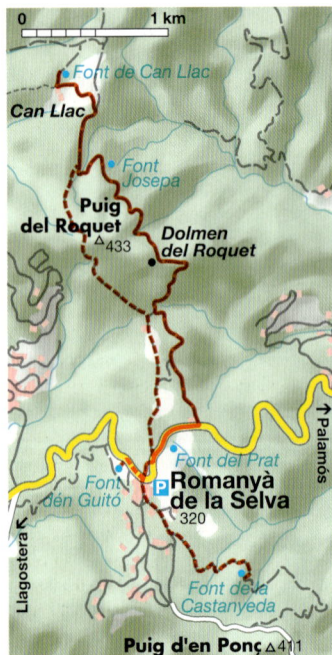

A geological fault in the nearby Gavarres Mountains is the reason why the environs of Romanyà de la Selva are blessed with a relatively abundant supply of water. This is the source for most of the springs included in this tour, which collect precious moisture for fields, farmsteads and villages. The walk connects a number of these ancient springs, one of which is the pleasantly situated Font Josepa, a nice shady spot to enjoy a picnic.

A lovely spot for a break: Font Josepa.

At the village limits of **Romanyà de la Selva**, the trail sign at the side of the road points out the GR 92-1 heading towards »Coll del Matxo Mort«. The path leads to a large stone cross, bends right and then returns to the main road. Turn left onto this and after about 100 metres reach the sign »Font del Prat«; turn right to reach the ivy-covered spring complex. Return to the main road and turn right to continue, passing Romanyá's cemetery (»Cementiri«). 50m past this, fork left onto a forestry road. With a view of the densely wooded Gavarres mountain range to the north, begin a pleasant ascent, later on descending easily for a while. At the sign for »Font Josepa«; turn right to reach the spring and a picnic table with a bench under the shade of a tree. Continuing along the trail, meet a wide forestry road marked with the trail sign »Coll del Matxo Mort«. Turn right here to reach an expansive clearing with sloping fields and the handsome farmstead Can Llac. Turn left away from the forestry road and onto the driveway leading to the farmstead. Once there, a little stretch to the right leads to the **Font de Can Llac**, 320m, surrounded by stately trees.

32 Along the Camí de Ronda between land and sea

First-hand impressions of the wild coast

Platja d'Aro – Torre Valentina and back

Starting point: Platja d'Aro, 0m, at the northern end of the Platja Llarga. Driving along the C-253 from Palamós, turn left at the second roundabout onto the Travessia del Caval Bernat until the street ends. Park there.

Walking times: Platja d'Aro – Torre Valentina 1¼ hrs, return 1¼ hrs; total time 2½ hrs.

Ascent: About 50m.

Grade: Easy walk.

Trail markings: The GR-92 (white/red).

Refreshment: Platja d'Aro.

Map: Baix Empordà-Sud (Mapes topogràfics), 1:30,000 (Editorial Piolet).

Information: Oficina de Turisme Platja d'Aro; Calle Mossèn Cinto Verdaguer, 11; ✆ 972.817179.

Notice: In the Spring of 2004, a stretch of the Camí de Ronda was closed because some of the trail had fallen away. According to the tourist office, the trail will be repaired again. For information regarding the current situation, contact the tourist office. When the sea is calm, however, this stretch can be avoided by skirting around along the rocky seashore – see the walk description.

Tip: The quiet hamlet of Castell d'Aro with its castle grounds is worth a visit.

The coastline between Platja d'Aro and Sant Antoni de Calonge as seen from above: always near the seashore, over beach and along cliffs, past inlets and islands – a Camí de Ronda par excellence. This is an easy, leisurely ramble, ideal for gazing at the scenery and includes a number of lovely spots for a dip in the sea; the perfect tour for a temporary escape from »beach life« on the Gran Platja.

Starting at the car park in **Platja d'Aro**, a few strides lead to the sandy beach. At the trail sign for the GR-92, head north in the direction of »Torre Valentina«. The fortified trail follows the coastline in continuous up-and-down walking, over steps and through pedestrian tunnels. Sometimes high above the sea, sometimes on the shoreline of sandy beaches or small inlets, then past the island of Belladonna Grossa lying just a little offshore, finally reach the Cap Roig promontory, formed from red-toned rock (hence the name: literally »red cape«). A little boathouse announces the bay with the unmistakeable inscription »Port de Cap Roig«. A little further on, the trail leaves the rocky seashore behind to ascend left along the slope. It is also possible, if the sea is calm and in case the damaged stretch of trail has not yet been repaired (see Notice), to scramble over the boulders at the shoreline and, on the other side, to take the steps on the left back to the Camí de Ronda. At another tight spot that follows, the GR skirts around by making a short ascent along the slope of the coastal cliff, passes a lovely viewing point and then descends again to the beach (here too, if the sea is calm, you can keep walking along the seashore). Pass the Treumal campsite, then through a pedestrian tunnel and after yet another delightful little inlet, reach the Cap de Roques Planes – literally: »cape of the flat rocks«. The trail skirts to the left around the cape that juts far into the sea, and then ascends over steps. The ancient watchtower Torre des Perpinyà comes into view – a great place to take in Palamós with its extensive bay. Continuing along the GR and back to the beach, meet up with the **Torre Valentina**. The sprawl of a huge apartment complex provides a modern contrast to the 16th-century defensive tower.

At the starting point: an information board sparks interest.

33 Carcaixells d'en Cama and Puig Montclar, 406m

An adventurous walk on the granite cliffs of the Ardenya

Starting point – Pas de la Canaleta – Puig Montclar and back

Starting point: The track to Can Llaurador, 50m. From Sant Feliu de Guíxols along the C-65 to Santa Cristina d'Aro; after driving through the village, turn left onto the GIV-6611 towards Solius; turn left in front of the Mas Pla (white/red GR markings) and cross over the Riera de Solius. Immediately after, turn right onto the wide dirt road until reaching the track bearing off to the left and marked by trail signs.

Walking times: Starting point – Pas de la Canaleta 1¾ hrs, Pas de la Canaleta – Puig Montclar ¾ hr, return 2 hrs; total time 4½ hrs.

Ascent: About 380m.

Grade: Sure-footedness, an excellent head for heights and scrambling experience are required. A number of stretches follow steep cliffs with safety cables.

Trail markings: The GR-92-1 (white/red); the PR-C-102 (white/yellow); a local walking trail (white/green).

Refreshment: None en route; Santa Cristina d'Aro.

Map: Baix Empordà-Sud (Mapes topogràfics), 1:30,000 (Editorial Piolet).

Information: Oficina de Turisme Santa Cristina d'Aro; Pl. Mossèn Baldiri i Reixac; ✆ 972.837010.

Alternative: Puig Montclar but without the ascending stretches through the Carcaixells. There are two variations: either along the PR-C-102 to Collet del Montclar or, the shorter version (though with steep ascents) along the white/green-marked »Sender local«: this trail forks off to the right about 400m along

the PR-C-102 and then ascends to Pas de la Canaleta.

Like a mountainous island split up into sheer and delightfully-formed rocky domes, the Serra de Montclar rises out of the flat surrounding countryside. One of the most attractive trails in the Baix Empordà can be walked here – leading through beautiful Mediterranean forests with full-grown strawberry trees, along ingeniously-constructed cliff trails and finally, over a suspension bridge to reach a startling panoramic peak. A few »acrobatic« interludes along well-secured stretches at the rim of the Carcaixells provide just the right ingredients to add a little excitement.

At the track, follow the **trail sign** for »El Montclar«. After passing the Can Llaurador, meet up with a signed junction and leave the GR 92-1 behind by heading straight ahead and following the PR-C-102 for a while, surrounded by a lovely wood mixed with pine, cork oak, eucalyptus and strawberry trees. Pass the Menhir de Can Llaurador, ignore the following track that forks left and, at a brook, reach a signed junction for the trail. Leave the PR-C-102 behind; this continues straight ahead and ascends to »Collet de Montclar« (→ Alternative). Turn right instead to continue along the white/green-marked »Sender local«. Cross over the brook and ascend along the narrow path through dense undergrowth to reach a little rocky saddle with a small chapel and a route plan for the rugged Carcaixells.

The »trail« that follows is an up-and-down, over-and-under route between towering crags and domes; this is hard to discern and seems to disappear from time to time – the white/green markings, however, lead faithfully on. Along the exposed stretches of the cliffs, chains are provided for a handhold. At the Pas dels Aritjols, reach the suspension bridge spanning a deep gorge and, afterwards, a signed trail junction: to the left, a precipitous path leads to »Pas de la Miloca«. Turn right, however, towards »Pas de la Canaleta«. A slight ascent is followed by a descent, part of which is along a cliff – a rope is provided for a handhold – and finally reach the inconspicuous **Pas de la Canaleta**, 334m.

Pay attention here: the trail that immediately descends from the little saddle returns to the PR-C-102 (→ Alternative). Instead, turn sharp right (cairns and coloured markings on stone) and head directly towards the tall power pylons and the trail signs at a forestry road. Now follow the signs for »Collet de Montclar« / »El Montclar« to meet up with the PR-C again at another saddle. Turn right, following the white/yellow markings to climb (a short stretch over boulders) to the nearby dome of the **Puig Montclar**, 406m, with a flagstaff and flag at the summit.

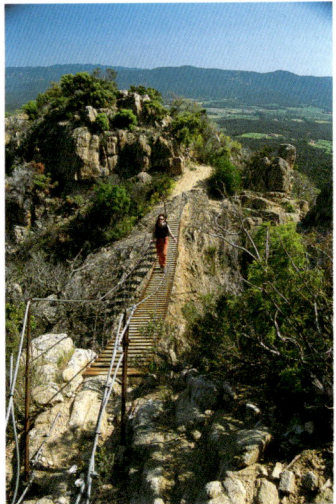

Suspension bridge in the Carcaixells.

34 Through the Ardenya, near the coast

At the gates of Sant Feliu de Guíxols

Sant Feliu de Guíxols – Coll de Portes – Sant Feliu de Guíxols

Starting point: The western end of the seaside promenade of Sant Feliu de Guíxols, 0m, at the signpost pointing out »St. Elm« / »St. Grau d'Ardenya« (PR-C-101).

Walking times: Sant Feliu de Guíxols – Coll de Portes 1½ hrs, Coll de Portes – Sant Feliu de Guíxols 1½ hrs; total time 3 hrs.

Ascent: About 160m.

Grade: Short stretches of strenuous ascent.

Trail markings: The PR-C-101 (white/yellow); a local walking trail (white/green) and the GR-92 (white/red).

Refreshment: None en route; Sant Feliu de Guíxols.

Map: Baix Empordà-Sud (Mapes topogràfics), 1:30,000 (Editorial Piolet).

Information: Oficina de Turisme Sant Feliu de Guíxols; Plaça Monestir; ✆ 972.820051.

Tip: The steep and winding coastal road (GI-682) between Sant Feliu de Guíxols and Tossa de Mar is worth driving. Along the panoramic route, this stretch of steep coastline is one of Costa Brava's most rugged and virtually undeveloped. Cyclists find the almost traffic-free road very attractive.

View of the broad, curved bay of Sant Feliu de Guíxols.

The coastline south of Sant Feliu de Guíxols presents yet again the spectacular side of the Costa Brava, before levelling out past Lloret de Mar and continuing straight on as endless sandy beach. The walk begins on the beach at the genial, unpresumptuous little seaside city and then climbs to the church of Sant Elm. On the way, enjoy great views of the coast reaching all the way to the castle of Tossa de Mar when the weather is clear. The route then turns inland to enter the wooded interior and cuts along the Vall de Mascanada, cultivated with gardens and fields – a quaint, idyllic spot lying just before the gates of the bustling village.

Starting at the **trail sign** and heading for »St. Elm«, at first walk along the coastal road then turn left onto a Camí de Ronda, continuing steadily on above the coastline. At a signpost, return to the main road and then along the ascending dirt road that meets up with a tarmac road at the end. Directly opposite, a trail makes a short cut to avoid a bend in the road, then turn right onto the road and ascend to a trail sign. Turn left following the sign for the *ermita* of Sant Elm, a lovely viewing point high above the sea.

Return to the signpost and turn right to continue on the main road; on the way, ignore a coast path descending to »Cala del Vigatà«. Almost a kilometre further on, cross over the GI-682 and follow the signs for »Coll de Portes« along a woodland path through pine and cork oak. Cross over a track and continue on to reach the **Coll de Portes**, 130m, and a trail junction. Stay a little longer on the PR-C towards »Vall de Mascanada« (turning right returns rapidly – white/green markings – to Sant Feliu de Guíxols) and at the following junction, turn right along the narrower, ascending forestry road to reach yet another fork. Here, leave the PR-C that leads to »Sant Benet« by taking the white/green-marked trail towards »Vall de Mascanada«. The delightful trail through dense vegetation merges with a forestry road; turn right here and pass a tall cliff on the right-hand side of the trail (at the top, enjoy a spectacular view of the bay of Sant Feliu de Guíxols!). Now, pass the Font del Pastor situated on the left. The extremely rutted forestry road then descends quickly into the Vall de Mascanada and crosses over the Riera de les Comes near a farmstead. Here, meet up with the GR-92 and follow this track through the valley. At the village limits, continue straight on along the tarmac road then turn diagonally right. Now, without further deviation, head directly to the sea and return to the broad **seaside promenade**.

35 Puig de ses Cadiretes, 518m

Tossa de Mar's highest mountain

Parc sa Riera – Mare de Deu – Puig de ses Cadiretes and back

Starting point: Parc sa Riera, 20m. Starting at Tossa de Mar, drive in the direction »Llagostera«. At the village limits, follow the signs for »Parc sa Riera«, pass the soccer field and then along a concrete overpass, cross the Riera de Tossa. Just on the other side, there are parking places near a little man-made wetland area (»Aiguamolls«).

Walking times: Parc sa Riera – Mare de Déu de Gràcia 1 hr, Mare de Déu de Gràcia – Puig de ses Cadiretes 1½ hrs, return 2 hrs; total time 4½ hrs.

Ascent: 500m.

Grade: A long hike with strenuous stretches of ascent; some sections of descent are slippery!

Trail markings: The white/red-marked GR-92 as well as numerous trail signs.

Refreshment: None en route, Tossa de Mar.

Map: Selva (Mapa comarcal de Catalunya 34), 1:50,000 (ICC).

Information: Oficina de Turisme in Tossa de Mar, Avenida del Pelegrí; ✆ 972.34 0108.

Alternative: The route can be extended to a **circular walk**. Return to the trail sign and turn left towards »Tossa per Vall de Roca«. The dirt road descends steeply and is sometimes slippery due to the sandy surface! All junctions are well-marked with trail signs or posts (at a right-angled fork with two small oak trees in the middle, bear left). At the end, pass Tossa's sewage treatment plant and rub-

bish dump to return to Parc sa Riera. Total time for the circular walk 4½ hrs.

Tip: Of course, Tossa de Mar itself, with an old town centre (Vila Vella) and a sprawling castle grounds above the sea, puts Tossa high on the list of the Costa Brava's most beautiful villages.

The verdant mountain ranges inland from Tossa de Mar climb rapidly in elevation and reach a height of more than 500 metres above sea level at the Puig de ses Cadiretes. The little rocky summit only peeks over the dense forests but just enough to open up a grand panoramic view of land and sea!

The ruins of the Mare de Déu de Gràcia chapel.

From the car park at the **Parc sa Riera**, take the road along the »Aiguamolls« and then cross over the brook flowing to the right. Past the bridge, turn immediately left on the road to reach a junction with a trail sign (this is the spot where the Alternative route returns). Bear right towards »Puig de ses Cadiretes«, climbing steeply up the sandy road. First reach the Coll del Sastre (inscription on a rock beneath two pine trees) and continue to the »Pins del Bispe« (inscription on a rock). After yet another fork with a signpost, meet up with a major trail junction where, to the right, »Cala de Giverola« is marked. Turn left, however, and reach the chapel **Mare de Déu de Gràcia**, 250m – only some scattered walls remain to mark the spot. Here, take the road right to ascend to the junction for »Sant Grau«; bear left, following the direction pointed out by the sign. At the next fork bear left, and yet again at the fork thereafter (GR markings on a rock as well as a wooden post indicate the direction). Past a lovely spot to take a break under the shade of some boulders, the road forks again: the »Montllor« mountain is pointed out to the left but continue straight ahead and soon reach a circular clearing with tall pine trees. Leave the GR which descends to »Sant Feliu de Guíxols« by bearing left. Continue on to the next signpost where a path forks off to the left and, after a few minutes, ends at the foot of the craggy peak. After a few scrambles over large boulders, set foot on the **Puig de ses Cadiretes**, 518m, which sports a cross (a firewatcher's tower is next to it).

Parc Natural del Montseny

On this side, the long and level coastline between Lloret de Mar and Barcelona, so straight as to appear drawn with a ruler – on that side, the Montseny with mountains reaching heights more than 1700m and only 30 km away from the seashore. The name »Montseny« comes from the Catalan »mont senyal« and in translation means »the mountain that can be seen from far away«. It is certain that this massif catches the eye from many regions of Catalonia, and no wonder, since the other mountain ranges in the »Serralada Prelitoral Catalana« are significantly lower in height. For this reason, Catalans consider Montseny a landmark and an ascent to the highest peak pays homage to the distinction.

Two roads crossing mountain passes divide the 30,000 hectares of the natural park, traversing the Coll de Sant Marçal to the east and the Coll Formic to the west. Both passes are situated over 1000m above sea level and are important starting points for opening up the interior of Montseny. Along the connecting line between the two passes, the Matagalls (Walk 37), at almost 1700m, is predominant; the name itself carries a variety of meanings. The massif juts out from the landscape in every direction and, because of its cen-

The Cingles de Bertí; in the background, the Montseny range.

tral location, counts as one of the most popular walking destinations in the area. The flat summit boasts a large cross and, on the second Sunday in July, a pilgrimage is made here. Of course, this is not the only reference point for religious fervour in a mountain range that has sheltered hermits and penitents since early on. One of these was Sant Segimon and the 13th-century monastery built on the steep northern flanks of the Matagalls is named after him (Walk 36). In a terribly ruinous condition not many years ago, the picturesquely-situated complex is now being restored as a concession to the needs of so many visitors; in addition to a refugi, a restaurant is planned to open.

A landmark of another kind is provided by the two highest summits of the Montseny near Santa Fe – both are at exactly 1706m and neighbour one another. A tarmac track leads to the Turó de l'Home, topped by a

Beech forest on the Turó de l'Home.

broadcast aerial and a weather station. Apparently, the track served as reason enough for mountain-view-hungry tourists to pack into cars and storm the peak because now the approach has been restricted for vehicles. The real destination for walkers is Les Agudes (Walk 38) at the end of a ridge promontory with an unrestricted 360°-view. Trails ascend here from different sides: from Coll de Sant Marcal along the scree-covered west flank, from the north along the most direct and currently exposed ridge ascent or from the Font de Passavets in the east, along slopes with delightful beech forests.

Also in the western region of the natural park, a nature track can be driven up to the relatively lower Tagamanent; the final metres to the summit platform, however, must be negotiated on foot. Here, too, are walking alternatives such as the tranquil GR trail from Aiguafreda (Walk 39). On the other side of the Congost Valley, across from Tagamanent and somewhat outside of the natural park boundaries, steep, sheer cliffs are found, the Cingles de Bertí (Walk 40). The extensive range provides a striking scenic contrast to the broad mountain domes of Montseny, from the rim of the Cingles, seeming so near, and at the same time, worlds apart.

36 Santuari de Sant Segimon, 1230m

A shrine in the midst of spectacular scenery

Coll Formic – Sant Segimon and back

Santuari de Sant Segimon.

Starting point: The Coll Formic, 1144m, on the BV 5301 between Seva and Montseny.

Walking times: Coll Formic – Sant Segimon 1½ hrs, back 1¼ hrs; total time 2¾ hrs.

Ascent: About 230m.

Grade: Easy walk.

Trail markings: None; forestry road.

Refreshment: None en route (a restaurant is planned to open in Sant Segimon); bar and restaurant on the Coll Formic.

Map: E-25, Montseny (Parc Natural), 1:25,000 (Editorial Alpina).

Information: Oficina del Parc Natural in El Brull; ✆ 93.8840692.

Alternative: Sant Miquel dels Barretons, 1300m. Perched on a sheer granite cliff at the back of the Santuari, the chapel presents wide-open views. At the cliff chapel of Sant Segimon, head to the right to pick up a steep path that winds up along the eastern side of the rock cliff; there and

back ½ hr.

Combination possible: With Walk 37 – Matagalls.

Tip: The information centre for the natural park is in El Brull.

The Montseny Mountains have been a place of refuge for hermits since early times. In the 6th century Segimon de Borgonya, who was later canonized, reportedly did penance for a number of years in the cave in the cliff where the chapel was later built. This acted as the cornerstone for the grand cloister complex that travellers at the end of the 19th century described as a comfortable place for lodging. Up until today, only ruins have remained. Admirably constructed on the steep northern flanks of the Matagalls foothills, the Santuari is now being restored and houses a refugí and a restaurant.

On the **Coll Formic**, head north-east along the ascending GR-5.2 until reaching a track. Turn right onto this and descend, passing a magnificent oak tree, and then meet up with the Mas de Santandreu. Past the sprawling farmstead, the track ascends, takes a sharp hook westwards, crosses over the GR and then heads north. Ignore a track forking right to Turó d'en Besa, as well as the following one that forks left. Making a switchback, the track drops down into the valley and, after crossing the stream, heads down the valley again. Just past an iron gate, cross a secondary valley by walking upstream and over, then pass the Font de Sant Miquel del Sant to the right of the trail. Near a wrought-iron cross on a rock, the track bends to the right and the church tower of the cloister comes into view. The track ends at the **Santuari de Sant Segimon**, 1230m. Through the gate and past the buildings, the cliff chapel can be found (→ Alternative); just next to it is a terrace with a wonderful, panoramic view.

109

37 Matagalls, 1696m

One of Montseny's classic tours

Coll Formic – Matagalls – Coll Saprunera – Coll Formic

Starting point: The Coll Formic, 1144m, on the BV 5301 between Seva and Montseny.
Walking times: Coll Formic – Matagalls 1¾ hrs, Matagalls – Coll Saprunera ¾ hr, Coll Saprunera – Coll Formic 1 hr; total time 3½ hrs.
Ascent: About 600m.
Grade: A moderately difficult walk with some strenuous ascents. Special care is required during fog.
Trail markings: GR-5.2 (white/red) until Matagalls; then unmarked along open terrain.
Refreshment: None en route; there is a bar and a restaurant on the Coll Formic.
Map: E-25, Montseny (Parc Natural), 1:25,000 (Editorial Alpina).
Alternative: Santuari de Sant Segimon,

1230m. From the Coll Saprunera, make a slight ascent and skirt left around the small summit of the Turó de Coll Saprunera, then descend along the ridgeline towards the rocky Turó de Sant Miquel and skirt around this to the right. Afterwards, reach the precipitously-perched Sant Miquel dels Barretons chapel and then take a very steep path down to the Santuari Sant Segimon. Return along the track to reach the descending trail from Coll Saprunera. Add about 1 hr to the tour.
Information: Oficina del Parc Natural in El Brull; ✆ 938.840692.
Tip: The little village of Montseny along the scenic BV-5301 leading to the pass is very popular with tourists.

One of the classic tours in the middle of the Montseny Natural Park, accessible from all sides on foot and very popular at the weekend, the walk takes the leisurely approach from the west and ends at the benign summit dome, where a first-rate view of the surrounding mountains can be enjoyed. Along the return route, the walker can visit the historical cloister grounds of the Santuari de Sant Segimon.

On the **Coll Formic**, take the GR and ascend north-eastwards; soon cross over a track and, in the same direction, climb steeply along the slope to reach another track. Cross over this track as well, and then the trail levels out along the slopes of the Turó d'en Besa. Past the first small saddle, the trail skirts around the only slightly higher Turó del Pla de la Barraca and afterwards reaches the saddle of the same name, 1367m, on lush, hilly pastureland. To the left of the trail, a

Matagalls, summit cross.

funnel-shaped depression catches the eye. Do not be led astray by the white/red-marked hook to the left, instead follow the eroded traces of trail that ascend directly along the western slope of the Turó Gros de Santandreu. The trail keeps left and below the summit dome; just in front, the Matagalls comes into view, sporting a cross on the summit. At about the same height, the trail cuts through the following summit dome of the Turó de l'Estanyol and then reaches the Collet dels Llops, 1565m. Now turning north-east, the final »push to the peak« begins: along a broad, rocky slope, follow markings to reach the **Matagalls**, 1696m, with a large summit cross.

On the return route, head westwards along the ridgeline. Although without markings, it is no problem to continue if you keep to the ridgeline along the chain of hills and from time to time some traces and ruts appear. At first descend slightly to the grassy Collet de la Font, ascend again onto the gentle dome that follows and then onwards to the Pla dels Ginebres, a lovely grassy plain dotted with juniper bushes. Continue along the ridge which now bends towards the north-west; finally, descend to the clearly discernable **Coll Saprunera**, 1393m, with a sign »Area Privada de Caza«. From here, the trail heads straight on to Sant Segimon (→ Alternative), however, to reach the Coll Formic descend left from the saddle along the wide cow path to climb down to a track. Turn left along the track, cross a tributary brook and into the lovely main valley. Now pass an iron gate and then reach a sharp bend in the track. Cross the valley stream and the brook following just after and immediately turn left onto a path that ascends along the brook and through open wood. Pass a craggy tower with a stone table and then, near an enclosed spring with a wrought-iron cross, reach grassy slopes dotted with bushes. Here the western slope of the Turó Gros de Santandreu, climbed just before, comes back into view. Now heading southwards through open terrain, meet up again with the ascending trail on the Pla de la Barraca. Turn right to return to the **Coll Formic**.

38 Turó de l'Home, 1706m, and Les Agudes, 1706m

The Montseny's landmarks

Passavets – Turó de l'Home – Les Agudes – Passavets

Starting point: The car park at the Font de Passavets, 1195m, at km 22 on the BV 5114 between Sant Celoni and Viladrau.

Walking times: Passavets – Turó de l'Home 1½ hrs, Turó de l'Home – Les Agudes ½ hr, Les Agudes – Passavets 1¼ hrs; total time 3¼ hrs.

Ascent: About 570m.

Grade: Sometimes strenuous ascents but overall not a difficult walk.

Trail markings: Green metal posts with rust-coloured markings until Turó de l'Home; from there until the Coll de Les Agudes along the GR-5.2 (white/red); the return route is marked in red.

Refreshment: None en route; Santa Fe.

Map: E-25, Montseny (Parc Natural), 1:25,000 (Editorial Alpina).

Information: The Centre d'Informació Can Casades in Santa Fe; ✆ 938.475113.

Notice: The approach along the road to Turó de l'Home is restricted to only a few vehicles. For the three car parks in the area of the summit, a maximum of only 50 vehicles is permitted.

Tip: The pilgrim's chapel of Santa Fe (early 13th century) is worth a visit. Starting from here, a short ramble can be undertaken through the beech and chestnut forests surrounding the Turó de Morou. The circular route »L'empedrat de Morou« is marked in orange and takes about 2 hrs to walk.

On the way to the Les Agudes summit.

Of the same height and in the same neighbourhood, nevertheless worlds apart – this is a succinct description of the impression gained when comparing the Montseny's highest peaks. While the walker will usually take only a brief stroll on the Turó e l'Home, modernised by road access and a broadcasting station, he is likely to take his time on the summit of Les Agudes, which is accessible along a delightful ridgeline trail, to enjoy the superb sweeping view of the natural park's mountains. The marvellous beech forests passed through along the way is a hiking adventure in itself, especially during the colourful autumn season.

At the car park **Font de Passavets**, take the marked forestry road and soon pass the nearby spring. Along easily ascending bends, climb up through the beech forest. Keep to the main trail and, at the end, head straight for the Turó de l'Home with its weather station; to the right, the ridge stretching to Les Agudes can be seen. The trail ascends to the road with the car park on the Coll Pregon; from here take the stepped trail up to the meteorological station on the **Turó de l'Home**, 1706m. The summit, only a little further up, is closed to protect the environment but can be circled around to take a look. Now descend from the entrance of the weather station along the wide terraced slope towards the ridge and to the road. Continue from there by turning right along the marked GR trail to traverse the slope of the ridge (as an alternative, climb directly to the ridgeline and continue on to Turó del Catiu d'Or, then follow the ridgeline path that merges later with the GR). In front of the protruding hump of the Puig Sacarbassa, the GR meets up with the ridge and skirts around along the left flank. After a short stretch on the scree-covered slope, reach the Coll de les Agudes, 1647m, where the return route forks off. The GR descends left from the saddle; however, follow the unmarked but distinct trace for the final metres to reach **Les Agudes**, 1706m, with a cross at the summit.

Return to the Coll de les Agudes and fork left from the saddle onto the descending rutted trail clearly marked in red. The trail climbs down through slopes of beech, sometimes along forestry paths, sometimes footpaths. On the way, pass the splendidly situated Font de Briançó. The trail ends at the road (the BV 5114) on the opposite side of the building »El Convent«; turn right here to return to the car park at the **Font de Passavets**.

39 Tagamanent, 1059m

Along the »Ruta Verdaguer« to one of the best viewing points in the Montseny massif

Aiguafreda – Collet de Sant Martí – Tagamanent and back

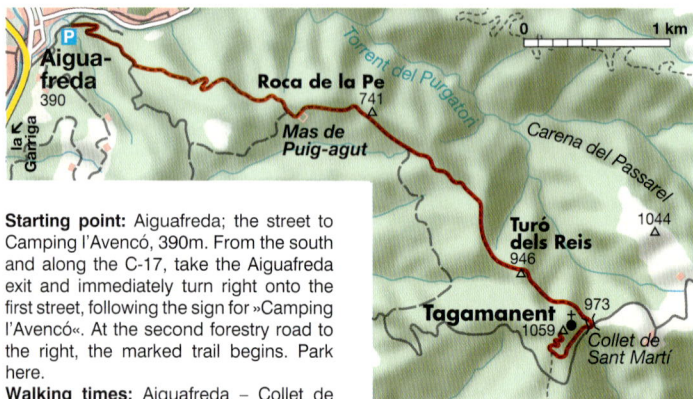

Starting point: Aiguafreda; the street to Camping l'Avencó, 390m. From the south and along the C-17, take the Aiguafreda exit and immediately turn right onto the first street, following the sign for »Camping l'Avencó«. At the second forestry road to the right, the marked trail begins. Park here.

Walking times: Aiguafreda – Collet de Sant Martí 1¾ hrs, Collet de Sant Martí – Tagamanent ¼ hr, return 1¾ hrs; total time 3¾ hrs.

Ascent: 669m.

Grade: A moderately difficult walk using ascents that are generally spaced at comfortable intervals; the ascent to the peak is more strenuous.

Trail markings: The GR-5 (white/red) until the Collet de Sant Martí; the ascent to Tagamanent along a distinct trail.

Refreshment: None en route; Aiguafreda.

Map: E-25, Montseny (Parc Natural), 1:25,000 (Editorial Alpina).

Information: The Oficina del Parc Natural in Figaró; ✆ 938.429361.

Tip: Mountain bikers will find the forestry road starting at the hamlet of Tagamanent (only a few kilometres south of Aiguafreda) and leading to the Collet de Sant Martí an interesting and challenging ride that can be extended along the mountain range »La Calma« to the Coll Formic.

Although only moderate in height, the Tagamanent presents a first-class panoramic view when the weather is clear. The summit plateau is crowned by the somewhat pretentious Santa Maria church but offers a number of cosy spots for a pleasant picnic with nice views of the area. Expect company at the weekend but not necessarily along the tranquil trails leading through the pretty forests; most of the visitors drive here on the forestry road from the hamlet of Tagamanent and only walk the last few metres to the summit.

Jutting viewing point on the Tagamanent.

At the beginning of the **forestry road**, a green metal post with GR markings points out the trail. Climb up along the forestry road to reach yellow gate-posts; here turn left onto the trail leading through a dense mixed forest. In a leisurely ascent, climb up to a main power line; at a pylon, turn left onto a forestry road and then pass the old Mas de Puig-agut (ruins) nearby. The view to the south-east reveals the wooded Tagamanent crowned by the church.

A little later, in a slight right-hand bend, turn left onto a trail and, after crossing the forestry trail, return to this once more. Only a few paces to the right along the forestry trail, turn left again onto the other trail that touches the forestry road yet again and later crosses over an old track. After a stretch of level walking, this merges with a narrow track; take this straight on to a complicated junction. Turn left here.

Shortly after, continue through open terrain – ignore a forestry road forking right – to reach the **Collet de Sant Martí**, 973m, and the track ascending from the hamlet of Tagamanent. From the small saddle, a conspicuous foot-path forks off to the southern side of the summit dome and ascends in bends to **Tagamanent**, 1059m.

40 Cingles de Bertí

Circular walk along the ridge of sheer cliffs

Sant Pere de Valldaneu – Cingles de Bertí – Sant Pere de Bertí – Sant Pere de Valldaneu

Starting point: Sant Pere de Valldaneu, 460m. In Aiguafreda, follow the signs »Estación RENFE« to the railway station on the other side of the river. Past the station, the street becomes a wide concrete-paved road that ends at a dirt track. Turn left here and continue for about 1 km until reaching the church and cemetery of Sant Pere de Valldaneu. The route is marked with blue trail markings.

Walking times: Sant Pere de Valldaneu – Cingles de Bertí 1¼ hrs, Cingles de Bertí – Sant Pere de Bertí 1¼ hrs, Sant Pere de Bertí – Sant Pere de Valldaneu 1¾ hrs; total time 4¼ hrs.

Ascent: About 550m.

Grade: Long circular walk with a stretch of strenuous and steep ascents up to the Cingles.

Trail markings: The GR-5 (white/red) until Sant Pere de Bertí; afterwards, the PRC-33 (white/yellow). The GR markings along the first stretch are somewhat inadequate; yellow arrows help out at decisive points.

Refreshment: None en route; Aiguafreda.

Map: E-25, Montseny (Parc Natural), 1:25,000 (Editorial Alpina).

Information: Oficina del Parc Natural in Figaró; ✆ 938.429361.

Tip: The waterfall at Sant Miquel del Fai tumbles down a multi-stepped rock wall

surrounded by cliffs in a striking natural amphitheatre. This can be reached along the narrow valley road BV-1485 that turns off from the C-59 in Sant Feliu de Codines.

The Cingles de Bertí (see photo on p.106) form a long limestone cliff face with sheer drops to the Congost Valley. While the approach from the west side provides good access since the incline is fairly gentle, the east side offers only a few paths ascending to the broad ridge, where the walking is then leisurely with fascinating views. One choice is the ascent along the lovely GR-5 through the Valldaneu Valley.

From the Ermita **Sant Pere de Valldaneu**, continue along the road a little further, then turn right onto the marked path and just a few metres on, turn left onto the track with a grassy strip in the middle. At the white/red marking on a dry stone wall, turn right again onto a path ascending gently through cultivated terraces. This leads along a dry stone wall below a farmstead and then meets up with a wide forestry road; after only a few paces, leave this behind by turning right onto another forestry road. Immediately after crossing a brook, take the trail forking right (yellow markings) which a little later merges again with the forestry road. This ascends rapidly but before it drops slightly again, turn right onto a steeply ascending path. The climb up through the steep slopes of the Cingles begins here. The steadily ascending trail is water-eroded at the start; further up, the trail continues in steep bends, levels out for a short stretch and then, after a strenuous last climb, reaches the ridge of the **Cingles de Bertí**, 810m, a jutting plateau dotted with a couple of trees.

Here, bear left and take a wide road to circle around the wooded hump of the Puig Fred. The road soon ends and becomes a trail that leads along the sheer edge of the Cingles – to the right are fields with two farmsteads – and then reaches a signpost. The valley descent of the PRC-33 turns left towards Figaró, but continue straight ahead and along the cliff's edge, enjoying a view of the Montseny range on the other side. Ignore a fork on the right-hand side – the circular route will return here later on. In between, the route follows a track for a short stretch before meeting up with a junction of forestry roads. Here, continue straight ahead and, changing direction towards the south-west, reach a fork; turn right onto the track blocked by a chain. This turns northwards now and drops slowly to a point near the **Sant Pere de Bertí** chapel, 820m.

In a sweeping left-hand bend, where the track drops down to the chapel, fork off right onto the narrow path of the PRC-33 in the direction of »La Trona«. This ascends along the slopes of the Cingles ridge, passes a large tumbledown farmstead and merges with an old track; turn left to follow this to a wide forestry road and then turn right onto the road to climb up through a forest. As soon as this begins to descend, turn right onto the marked path through the wood. This leads above the Font del Pollancre and passes a water basin, at the same elevation of which, you have to turn right onto the narrower path. Now ascend to the wooded ridgeline. Turn left here and continue until reaching a clearing where a number of stone markers have been placed on the right-hand side of the trail. Leave the ridgeline behind by turning right and descending to a track; cross over this diagonally left and then pick up the trail again. Cross over another track, then the trail passes somewhat below and to the left of a farmstead, traverses terraces and crosses a rocky rut while climbing down to the trail leading along the rim of the Cingles. From here, return along the approach route to **Sant Pere de Valldaneu**.

Parc Natural Sant Llorenç del Munt i Serra de l'Obac

Built into a prominent overhang: El puig de la Balma.

Only a stone's throw from Barcelona, the road leading to the pass north of Terrassa divides the natural park, which is bordered by the Ripoll and Llobregat rivers, into two regions. To the west, the Serra de l'Obac with the fortress-like Castellsapera as the highest summit, and to the east, the mountainous region of Sant Llorenç del Munt, named after the Romanesque monastery that is enthroned atop of La Mola. At 1107m, La Mola is the highest mountain in the natural park and can be seen from far and wide but is not really a »peak« in the usual sense of the word. The name »La Mola« expresses this apparition very well: when driving up to the Coll d'Estenalles, La Mola appears as a »large, bulky mass« rising rather shapeless and plump out from the dense oak and pine forests. From closer up, the first impression is replaced by a much different one: here is a diverse mountain landscape, with broad, steep cliff faces, stone fortresses, deeply-indented fissures – and often inserted in between – solitary, bizarrely-formed, towering crags that act as grotesque monuments to erosion. A good example is the renowned Morral del Drac along the route to La Mola (Walk 43). Montcau, an extremely popular summit due to the view it takes in, presents a spellbinding massive heap of conglomerate rock in its purest form (Walk 42).

The mountains of the natural park belong to the Catalonian Serralada Prelitoral, a range stretching from the Pyrenees and through the coastal interior. These mountains were created in the Tertiary period from flooding rivers that left sedimentary rock as well as limestone and clay deposits, when combined, produced cement-like masses of solid rock. The steady effects of erosion finished up the final details on, and beneath, the surface of the rock cliffs: numerous caves were opened up or the base of cliffs were so undermined that gigantic roof-like overhangs were created. These formations provide the basic framework for the »balma«, wall-enclosed overhangs utilised for combined living quarters and for defence purposes. The most striking example is the multi-levelled »Puig de la Balma« from the Middle Ages and not far from the tastefully restored hamlet of Mura (Walk 41). This is located on the border of the almost 14,000 hectare natural park; in the confines of the protected nature reserve, there are no human settlements.

For the inhabitants of this once extensively cultivated mountain region, defence was a primary concern and not only against raids by feudal and ecclesiastical potentates. Some tracts were controlled by bands of robbers who made life difficult for travelling traders on the route between the Catalonian commercial centres of Barcelona and Manresa. The ancient trade route through the Serra de l'Obac is now a part of the hiking trail »Camí Ral«. The route to »Castellsapera« (Walk 45) passes a site that was notorious for frequent hold-ups.

When crossing the mountains in former times, not only the narrow valleys had to be negotiated, the criss-cross mountain ranges often presented barriers too. Many of these extensive »Carenas«, however, offered broad, level ridges as leisurely connecting routes without arduous climbing or dangerously exposed drops. Pleasant walks can be taken along these densely wooded ridges (Walk 44) and the panoramic views are in no way inferior to those taken in on the summits of the natural park's »peaks«.

41 Circular walk near Mura

Walk the scenic gamut of the Serra de l'Obac

Mura – Coves de Mura – El Cargol – Mura

Starting point: The Centre d'Informació in Mura at the village limits on the road towards Rocafort, 450m.
Walking times: Mura – Coves de Mura 1½ hrs; Coves de Mura – El Cargol 1 hr, El Cargol – Mura ¾ hr; total time 3¼ hrs. (without a visit to the caves).
Ascent: About 320m.
Grade: Not a difficult circular walk; some short stretches of strenuous ascent.
Trail markings: Red blazes on green metal posts.
Refreshment: None en route; Mura.
Map: E-25, Sant Llorenç del Munt i l'Obac (Parc Natural), 1:25,000 (Editorial Alpina).
Information: The Centre d'Interpretació on the Coll d'Estenalles; ☎ 938.317300. The Centre d'Informació in Mura (☎ 938.318375) is only open at the week-

end and on holidays.
Alternative: The excursion to both mountain springs, which takes a good half-hour of the total time, can be left out of the tour or undertaken separately along the trail (»Les fonts de Mura«) marked with green blazes; total time about 1½ hrs.
Notice: To visit the cave, a 200m deep horizontal cavity, a good head torch is required. Please be sure to close the entrance door! The short stretch along the stream bed of the Torrent d'en Reixac can be difficult to negotiate during periods of heavy rainfall.
Tip: El puig de la Balma. A delightfully situated farmstead complex with a large part of the edifice built into the face of an overhanging cliff. Dating as far back as the Middle Ages, the complex houses a little museum, which is open on Saturday and holidays from 10 – 12 am and 4 – 6 pm, otherwise, special arrangements can be made with the residents ☎ 93.7433274. A restaurant is also open at the weekend. Almost 2km past Mura and driving towards Rocafort, turn left onto the signed forestry road and continue for another 2km to reach the farmstead. Starting out from Mura at the Centre d'Informació, walk along the local trail (dark brown markings) to reach the farmstead on foot.

Entrance to the Coves de Mura.

The sensational circular walk in the mountains around the enchanting hamlet of Mura is, so to speak, a tapas bar for the scenic delicacies of the natural park; romantic springs, an open cave with lovely cliff formations, a bizarrely-eroded rock tower, shady forests and interesting views of nearby and far away mountain ranges such as Montseny and Montserrat.

Starting at the **Centre d'Informació**, cross over the Riera de les Nespres along a concrete-paved road and then turn left upstream for a short way until reaching a poultry enclosure (»La Grangeta«). Turn right here onto the ascending trail and, at a fork, turn right again to make the excursion to the first spring. The green-marked path leads above the stream to a large overgrown overhang, beneath which the Font La Mascarosa bubbles and gurgles. Return to the main trail and after a short ascent, meet up with a second fork that also turns right and after a few minutes reaches the Font de la Coma. After this, return and remain on the red-marked path from which the green and dark-brown marked trails soon split off. The rocky trail follows the Torrent de Reixac and, after a waterfall, approaches the stream and continues along the rocky stream bed only to leave it again 100m further on at a signpost.

Along an ascending path, cross over a forestry road and head through oak and pine woods with dense undergrowth. Below is the increasingly gorge-like and densely overgrown stream valley, and on the other side a splendid cliff face of conglomerate rock along which the return route will later lead. At a signpost, take the forest path to the left which quickly leads to the **Coves de Mura**, 680m.

Now go back to the main trail. Still ascending, the trail leaves the dense forest and continues through open and ever-rockier terrain. Here, a majestic view opens up of the natural park's mountain ranges and over to the Montserrat massif. Shortly past a signpost, bump into a wider trail that leads to the right towards »Coma d'en Vila«; turn left, however, and continue high above the valley, heading back and enjoying the view of the ponderous massif of the Montcau and the far-off Pyrenees. The trail drops down to pass the lovely Font Cargol, murmuring away in a mossy basin and, after a stretch of forest, reaches the bizarrely-eroded **El Cargol** crag, 700m. Now in a rapid descent, meet up with a forestry road; turn right to climb down to the little gardens near Mura and to the Riera de Nespres. Cross over a wooden footbridge, and then head downstream along the track. When this ends, turn right and enter the village to meet up with the main street at the Hostal de Mura. Turn left and follow the main street back to the **Centre d'Informació**.

42 Cova Simanya and Montcau, 1056m

A popular peak in the natural park Sant Llorenç del Munt

Coll d'Estenalles – Cova Simanya – Montcau – Coll d'Estenalles

View from the Cova Simanya.

Starting point: The Centre d'Interpretació on the Coll d'Estenalles, 873m. The pass is located at km 14,8 on the BV 1221 between Terrassa and Navarcles.
Walking times: Coll d'Estenalles – Cova Simanya ¾ hr, Cova Simanya – Montcau ¾ hr, Montcau – Coll d'Estenalles ¾ hr; to-

tal time 2¼ hrs (without a visit to the caves).
Ascent: About 240m.
Grade: Sure-footedness on cliffs is required; some strenuous stretches of ascent.
Trail markings: The GR 5 (white/red) until Coll d'Eres.
Refreshment: None en route; Mura and Matadepera.
Map: E-25, Sant Llorenç del Munt i l'Obac (Parc Natural), 1:25,000 (Editorial Alpina).
Information: The Centre d'Interpretació on the Coll d'Estenalles (10 am – 3 pm); ℂ 938.317300.
Combination possible: With Walk 43 to La Mola
Notice: The Cova Simanya can be explored using a strong head torch. The beautifully formed gallery is connected to another cave at the end but the entrance is too narrow to pass through. Artefacts found in the cave show evidence of inhabitation from the 5th – 4th centuries BC. Warning: during wet periods, exploration may be impossible without getting your feet wet.
Tip: Frequent visitors to Montcau have caused severe erosion to set in. Plans are in progress to reconstruct and provide markings for the trail; in the meantime, the park administration asks that you stick to the main trails and avoid shortcuts!

It is almost impossible to just pass by Montcau since the massive formation with its pyramid peak captures the eye from every direction. Montcau is certainly not a pretty mountain, but the sluggish contour lines of the surprisingly colourful conglomerate rock exude a peculiar attraction – like a shapeless, primeval ink-blot in rock that only upon closer inspection reveals the richness of its forms. Extend the short tour with an excursion to the Cova Simanya, one of the most important caves found in the natural park and easy to explore.
At the **Centre d'Interpretació**, take the tarmac track following the GR 5. This winds along the foot of the Montcau foothills and ascends to the Coll d'Eres,

942m. At the pleasant little spot sporting a monument to the Catalonian poet Joan Maragall, the trail splits into three. At first, remain on the GR 5, taking the middle fork that descends from the saddle diagonally to the left. The forest trail drops rapidly and then forks at a green metal post. Here, leave the GR by turning left and continuing along the foot of the rocky protuberance and high above the Canal del Llor with mostly level walking until reaching the signed **Cova Simanya**, 910m. The splendidly formed and colourful cave entrance can be easily climbed up to along the rock slope.

Back to Coll d'Eres, pick up the rocky trail to the right. Sparingly marked in purple, this climbs straight towards the Montcau while opening up a view to the right of the ravaged towering crags of the Care-

The pyramid peak of Montcau.

na dels Emprius. Exposed rocky terrain sometimes gives way to meagre scrub vegetation, until reaching the bare rock forming the peak; here, a metal post points out a trail forking off that will be used for the return. Continuing in the same direction (blue arrow), climb up the coarse surface of the rock (which provides good grip), to reach the summit of **Montcau**, 1056 m, marked by a column. Along the gentle dome of the summit, it is easy to continue a little northwards to enjoy a view of the fine formations of the neighbouring Roques de la Coca. Back to the summit, take the alternative path to the right, descending south-west and finally join the road again only a few minutes before returning to the **Centre d'Interpretació**.

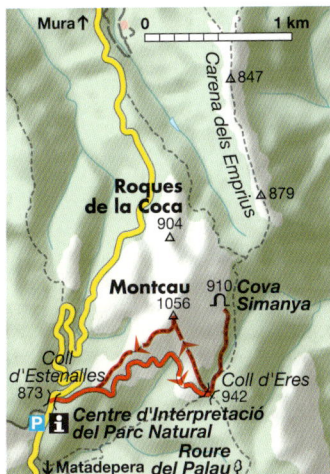

43 La Mola, 1107m

Unique and charming scenery along the way to the natural park's highest peak

Coll d'Estenalles – Morral del Drac – La Mola and back

Starting point: The Centre d'Interpretació on the Coll d'Estenalles, 873m. The pass is located at km 14,8 on the BV 1221 between Terrassa and Navarcles.
Walking times: Coll d'Estenalles – Morral del Drac 1½ hrs, Morral del Drac – La Mola ¾ hr, return 1¾ hrs; total time 4 hrs.
Ascent: About 360m.
Grade: A few strenuous stretches of ascent.
Trail markings: The GR 5 (white/red) until the Coll d'Eres; from there, green metal posts with orange blazes.
Refreshment: There is a restaurant at the Monestir Sant Llorenç del Munt; Mura and Matadepera.
Map: E-25, Sant Llorenç del Munt i l'Obac

(Parc Natural), 1:25,000 (Editorial Alpina).
Information: The Centre d'Interpretació on the Coll d'Estenalles, ✆ 938.317300 (open daily from 10 am – 3 pm), and the Informació del Parc on the cloister grounds on La Mola, ✆ 937.435454 (open daily 11 am – 3 pm).
Combination possible: With Walk 42 to Montcau.
Tip: A short excursion to Els Òbits, 1000m, is worthwhile; the fascinating living quarters with fortifications are built into a cliff and date from the Middle Ages. Along the marked path, turn left and follow a level trail for a few minutes to the extended overhang of the cliff face, enclosed by walls.

The highest point in the Sant Llorenç del Munt Natural Park is crowned by a Romanesque cloister bearing the same name. The approach for this popular walking destination follows a glorious ridge route and passes through beautiful forest along the Carena del Pagès, with sweeping views of the mountain formations and deeply-cut crevices dividing the cliffs.

Conglomerate rock characterises the natural park's landscape.

Begin at the **Centre d'Interpretació** and follow Walk 42 until reaching the Coll d'Eres, 942m. Here, turn right along the wide forestry road in a leisurely ascent, passing through a dense oak forest; on the way, pass the monumental »Roure del Palau«, a 30m high oak tree. At the following junctions, keep to the coloured trail markings and after a short descent, reach a marked path forking left that leads to »Els Òbits« (see Tip). Continue straight ahead and soon the bulky, stepped north face of La Mola comes into view. To the left, a view opens up of the Montseny Mountains and, in a level clearing to the right, enjoy a great view of Montserrat. The trail skirts around to the right of the Turó d'en Griera's summit and then takes a pronounced bend to the left, sometimes over exposed, rocky slopes and then again through forest to reach a small pass with the prominent rock monolith **Morral del Drac**, 970m. The crag has been beautifully sculpted by erosion and sports a cross at the top. (A secondary path leads left to the foot of the crag!) At the trail junction, a left turn leads to »Ermita de Santa Agnès« that can be reached in 10 minutes; the trail to the right descends through the narrow Canal de l'Abella to Can Pobla. Keep straight ahead, however, and head down the valley. A short stretch through a little wood is followed by a strenuous ascent for a couple of metres to a large boulder (with a red and white arrow) perched on a slab of rock. Pay attention now: past this point, a level trail continues straight ahead – do not follow this but instead climb diagonally left following a number of marked posts and aiming for the foot of the steep cliff face. From there, continue through dense forest and through a steep passageway in the rock (on the right-hand side, an enormous rock slab is leaning on the cliff face) along the open slopes above the cliffs' edge. Climb up the slope along the broad, rocky trace, cut through a little wood and then the grassy dome summit with the cloister appears; the trail ascends along this to **La Mola**, 1107m. A panoramic map provides orientation for the sweeping view, which even includes Mallorca if the weather is right.

44 Turó de la Pola, 929m

Pleasant tranquillity while walking along the GR high mountain trail

Coll d'Estenalles – Turó de la Pola and back

Starting point: The Centre d'Interpretació on the Coll d'Estenalles, 873m. The pass is located at km 14,8 on the BV 1221 between Terrassa and Navarcles.
Walking times: Coll d'Estenalles – Turó de la Pola 1½ hrs, return 1¼ hrs; total time 2¾ hrs.
Ascent: About 110m.
Grade: Easy walk.
Trail markings: The GR 5 (white/red).
Refreshment: None en route; Mura and Matadepera.
Map: E-25, Sant Llorenç del Munt i l'Obac (Parc Natural), 1:25,000 (Editorial Alpina).
Information: The Centre d'Interpretació on the Coll d'Estenalles; ✆ 938.317300 (open daily 10 am – 3 pm).
Alternative: Castellsapera, 939m. Before the Turó de la Pola, follow the GR-5 to the Coll de Tres Creus; here, the trail splits into three forks. Continue straight ahead and, at the fork immediately following, turn right, keeping on the GR-5 (the trail to the left approaches the Castellsapera along the eastern flank). Now through dense forest at the foot of the cliff face, continue to an open ridge along which the GR-5 descends straight ahead. Turn left, however, onto the path that immediately re-enters the forest and continue for about 200m until the trail's edge becomes rocky; the ascent to Castellsapera begins here to the left. Continue by referring to Walk 45.
Tip: The romantic Font de la Pola on the western slope of the Turó de la Pola is worth a visit. An extra half-hour's detour leads to the spring surrounded by oak

trees, after passing the Balma de la Porquerissa built into a cliff. Continue on the GR 5 to Coll de Tres Creus, then turn right onto the white/green marked path. Enjoy a spectacular view of Montserrat. After passing through dense forest, reach the Coll de la Porquerissa with the »cave« of the same name. Take a sharp bend to the north for about 5 minutes to reach a copse of holm oaks where a path forks off to the right and heads for the foot of the cliff face and the Font de la Pola.

As plain as the Turó de la Pola may seem, stuck in the middle of the fantastic rock formations of the Serra de l'Obac, the gentle rocky dome offers grandiose views over the natural park and far away. The approach is via a delightful high mountain trail, good for a leisurely ramble.

In a panoramic location: the little chapel of Sant Jaume.

On the **Coll d'Estenalles**, pick up the track across from the information office and signed for »La Mata«. This heads straight for the large building where the natural park administration is housed. In the left-hand bend in front of it, the GR turns off to the right (signpost), however, keep to the track for the moment. Directly in front of the administration building, climb up to the right to reach the picturesquely-situated little chapel of Sant Jaume, with Montcau as a backdrop.

Now descend on the other side to the forestry road to merge with the GR and stroll for a while along a boulevard-like way flanked by oak trees. Now the GR turns left to leave the track behind and follows a lovely trail along the ridgeline. Easy up, and easy down, over small saddles, this is a fairly level section, sometimes crossing through pleasant patches of forest and sometimes over exposed areas with changing views of Montserrat, La Mola and Montseny. At the end, meet up with the trail junction at the foot of the Turó de la Pola: the GR skirts to the left and around the summit and continues to Coll de Tres Creus (→ Alternative). However, head straight on along the narrow track and after a short, easy ascent, reach the »summit« of **Turó de la Pola**, 929m.

45 Castellsapera, 939m

Along the Camí Ral to the highest point of the Serra de l'Obac

La Barata – Castellsapera and back

In view: Castellsapera.

Starting point: At km 9 on the BV 1221 from Terrassa to Navarcles, 640m. Parking on the lay-bys on the shoulder of the road across from the buildings of the Mas la Barata.

Walking times: Car park – Castellsapera 1½ hrs, return 1¼ hrs; total time 2¾ hrs.

Ascent: 299m.

Grade: Sure-footedness for the very steep gully at the end of the walk and some scrambling skills are required.

Trail markings: Green metal posts with blue blazes (Camí Ral- markings); cairns during the final ascent.

Refreshment: None en route; Matadepera.

Map: E-25, Sant Llorenç del Munt i l'Obac (Parc Natural), 1:25,000 (Editorial Alpina).

Information: The Centre d'Interpretació on the Coll d'Estenalles; ✆ 938.317300 (open daily 10 am – 3 pm).

Alternative: Paller de Tot l'Any, 818m. At the path ascending to Castellsapera, head straight on to pick up the GR 5 (white/red) along the ridgeline. Take this to descend left through woods and over bare rock, passing the extremely jutting Roca Salvatge to finally reach the Collet Gran,

762m. Here, take the path forking left to ascend to the foot of the bulbous rocky peak; from the junction, there and back ¾ hr.

Tip: The permanent exhibition for the natural park »Sant Llorenç del Munt i Serra de l'Obac« in the Casal de Cultura in Matadepera, Pere Aldavert; ℂ 937.300132 (open workdays 10 am – 1 pm and 4 pm – 6 pm).

Like a fortress castle, the broad face of the Castellsapera rises out of the wooded mountain ranges of the Serra de l'Obac, presenting a sweeping open view in all directions. The following ascent leads along a section of the Camí Ral, once an important trading route between Barcelona and Manresa. The surroundings of Castellsapera were feared by travellers in the 16th and 17th centuries because of numerous bands of robbers prowling the area.

From the **car park**, take the road towards the Coll d'Estenalles for about 250m to meet up with the Camí Ral (signpost) turning left. Along the forestry trail soon meet up with an intersecting trail, follow this to the right and at the next major junction turn left. In an easy ascent, reach an intersecting trail again and turn left. At a small clearing, the Castellsapera appears for a moment, then the trail bends sharply left and leads again through forest with some open areas. Reaching open terrain and ascending over rocky ground, meet up with a green-marked fork to the left; however, continue straight ahead (sign for »Castellsapera« marked on a stone) and shortly after, end up at the Coll del Mal Pas del General, heralded by a signpost with two blazes. The sign points out that this stretch was once notorious for hold-ups. Now cross open terrain along the level trail and take in superb views of Montserrat; head straight towards the cliff »castle« in front of you. Back into the woods, reach a fork (yellow markings on a stone) and take the trail easily ascending to the right, passing through a short area of scrub and then re-enter a dense wood. Here, watch the trail's edge closely and when it becomes rocky, the ascending path, marked with cairns and blue signs, forks off to Castellsapera. This winds through a steep, wooded slope, climbing up to a cramped rocky gully where the ascent steepens for a short stretch. Reach a narrow saddle in a craggy passage (where a trail immediately descends again and leads to the Coll de Tres Creus). The little passage divides the summit platform; scramble up a few metres to the left or right to finally stand on the level »ramparts« of the **Castellsapera**, 939m, with lovely flora.

Parc Natural de Montserrat

At the highest point of Montserrat: view from Cim de Sant Jeroni.

Montserrat – this is the Garden of Eden before the gates of Barcelona, a bizarrely-eroded massif hard to compare with any other. Montserrat – here also is the hurly-burly of tourists targeted on the Benedictine monastery, set against the spectacular crag scenery, a legendary Catalonian pilgrimage place where busloads of visitors come to pay homage. Only a short distance away from the monastery grounds, the quietude of the mountains sets in. Even along the traditional trails to the highest peak, the Cim de Sant Jeroni (Walk 46), it is very possible on a workday that the walker will meet no-one else and enjoy the marvellous panoramic view in solitude. This is even more likely for the lesser-used trails. It is best to avoid random exploration, however; those not absolutely familiar with the multitude of paths and ascending trails that pass through these mountains can easily get lost in the tangle of overgrown gullies, valleys and crags. Some walkers have even disappeared here, so far-removed is Montserrat. Not without reason, during and after the Spanish Civil War, members of the resistance against the Franco regime chose this clandestine and confounding mountainous region as a refuge.

With an extraordinary variety of formations, Montserrat is not only a paradise for rock-climbers who can find all levels of challenge here; the walker is also treated to a panoptic spectrum of surreal rock formations: bizarre towers and needles, jagged rims and massive slabs can all be relished along an extensive network of trails. These are not mountains in the normal sense of the word, but rather an enchanted garden or a fantasy turned to stone. The names attached to these crags bear witness: from »L'Elefant« to »El Faraó«, everything is imaginable. The unique scenery has been created by the incessant erosion on the conglomerate gravel and limestone rock mixture that accumulated eons ago in the central Catalonian basin. Seen from the south, Montserrat – literally »serrated mountains« – with vineyards and olive groves making up the foreground, exudes a welcoming allure, while the north face presents a fortress-like image. The north face is broken up by a few steep gullies that allow access to the main range on foot. One of these presents an ascent to the very centre of Montserrat, the Montgrós (Walk 49): although not the highest, nonetheless the »summit« with best encompassing view open to the walker. From here, one gains a good impression of the heart of this »mountain island«. To the west, the Agulles (Walk 50) catch the eye, a fascinating ensemble of bunched-up crag needles puncturing the heavens. These are the favourite realm for rock-climbers who descend upon Montserrat in droves at the weekend and can be seen hanging everywhere on the rock faces. The mountains are bordered to the east by the Cim de Sant Salvador and the craggy Els Flautats, one of the most scenic groupings of rock formations; these can be explored along an exciting circular route (Walk 47). From the distance, Montserrat appears like a rocky isle, rising virtually uninhibited out of the flat surroundings. From on top, the impression is confirmed the other way round, like along the GR 172, hugging the foot of Montserrat's long, sunless north face or, even more lovely, along the panoramic trail through the Serra Llarga (Walk 48) above the Llobregat Valley.

Montserrat monastery.

46 Cim de Sant Jeroni, 1224m

Along old and new trails to Montserrat's classic peak

Plaça del Monestir – Capella de Sant Jeroni – Cim de Sant Jeroni and back

Starting point: Plaça del Monestir, 710m. The paying car park in front of the monastery grounds.
Walking times: Plaça del Monestir – Capella de Sant Jeroni 1¼ hrs, Capella de Sant Jeroni – Cim de Sant Jeroni ½ hr, return 1¼ hrs; total time 3 hrs.
Ascent: 514m.
Grade: Sometimes strenuous stretches of ascent.
Trail markings: A short stretch at the beginning along the GR 172-4 (white/red); signposts and aged yellow markings.
Refreshment: None en route; Bars and restaurants on the Plaça del Monestir.
Map: Montserrat (Parc Natural), 1:10,000 (Editorial Alpina).
Information: The Oficina de Turisme de Montserrat; ✆ 93.8777777.
Combination possible: With Walk 47: Els Flautats.
Alternative: The return route can be shortened by taking the rack railway »Funicular de Sant Joan« at the end of the »Camí Nou«.
Notice: From Monistrol, a rack railway (Cremallera) can be taken to the Monestir de Montserrat as well as a cable car from the railway station »Aeri de Montserrat«. Both enjoy good railway connections to and from Barcelona. Up-to-date schedules

are available through the tourist offices.
Tip: Be sure to pay a visit to the monastery.

Two trails lead to the highest peak of Montserrat (photo, pg.130), where a small viewing terrace is built on top. The »Camí antic« is the old approach through a long valley – under the shade of lush greenery to the little chapel of Sant Jeroni. The »Camí Nou«, built along the edge of the ridge of the Serra de les Paparres, presents a spectrum of delightful views taking in the oddly-formed needles and the massif of Montserrat. The superb view from the summit goes without saying! Although »the« classic tour, on weekdays the route is relatively quiet.

From the car park, take the road to **Plaça del Monestir**, continue to the last buildings and the end of the road. Here, climb up steps to a signpost »Sant Jeroni«; bear right, cross the little bridge spanning the dry gorge and begin the ascent along the »Pas dels Francesos«. The popular ascent through the narrow gorge leads over countless concrete steps and reaches the »Placeta de Santa Anna«, where the trail splits immediately after the final steps. Both the GR and a white/yellow marked trail turn right here, however continue straight ahead to reach yet another fork where the route back will return. Ignore the trail forking left (white/yellow marked) and take the trail forking right which continues with yellow markings. This ascends to the foot of the bulging »Panxa del Bispe« (in English: »bishop's paunch«) and drops down afterwards to a pleasant wood »Pla dels Ocells« sporting a stone obelisk. Follow the sign for »Sant Jeroni« and ramble pleasantly along the old stream bed (sometimes within the bed itself) through a marvellous forest often shading the trail. Now the trail leaves the stream bed and ascends in some bends to merge at a signpost with the »Camí Nou«, situated somewhat higher up; turn right to continue along the »Camí Nou«. Soon the trail widens and, after a short stretch over steps, reaches the **Capella de Sant Jeroni**, 1140m. In front of the chapel, turn sharp left and ascend a narrower trail; shortly after, the trail bends away northwards and climbs up fortified steps to the viewing platform at **Cim de Sant Jeroni**, 1224m.

Along the stepped descent, a nearby viewing terrace to the right presents a breathtaking view over the southern region of Montserrat. Continue on to the beginning of the »Camí antic« but keep to the »Camí Nou« above the valley and along the ridge of the Serra de les Paparres. The pleasant and mostly level trail offers striking views of the bizarre formations of the eastern region; now and again, paths fork off to the right to the Serra's ridgeline where views can be enjoyed of the rocky »islands« and cliff faces in the other direction. After climbing a few small steps near the cone-shaped monolith »Gorra Frígia«, the trail heads for the »Tebes« rock face and traverses the slope along a little rocky ravine; past this, the monastery grounds come into view. Now the trail drops steadily to an obvious right-hand bend where the summit station for the »Funicular de Sant Joan« (→ Alternative) suddenly appears. In the bend, turn off left onto the white/yellow-marked path and descend through forest to the stream bed. Continue to the other side and then ascend again, passing the ruins of the »Santa Anna« chapel, to meet up again with the approach trail. Turn right and along the »Pas dels Francesos« head back to the **Plaça del Monestir**.

47 Els Flautats

Circling the Cim de Sant Salvador

Plaça del Monestir – Pla de la Trinitat – Sant Salvador – Plaça del Monestir

Starting point: Plaça del Monestir, 710m. The paying car park in front of the monastery grounds.
Walking times: Plaça del Monestir – Pla de la Trinitat ¾ hr, Pla de la Trinitat – Sant Salvador 1¼ hrs; Sant Salvador – Plaça del Monestir ½ hr; total time 2½ hrs.
Ascent: About 430m.
Grade: Sure-footedness: the ascent along the Canal Plana is very steep.
Trail markings: The GR 172-4 (white/red) until the Canal Plana; later on, yellow markings.

Refreshment: None en route; there are bars and restaurants on the Plaça del Monestir.
Map: Montserrat (Parc Natural), 1:10,000 (Editorial Alpina).
Information: Oficina de Turisme de Montserrat; ✆ 93.8777777.
Combination possible: With Walk 46: Cim de Sant Jeroni.
Notice: See Walk 46.
Tip: The marvellous viewing point in front of the enormous crag for rock-climbers »L'Elefant« is a great place for a break.

An exciting itinerary full of surprises – this is a concise synopsis of the circular route around the massif of the Sant Salvador in the eastern region of Montserrat. Solitary high mountain trails with fantastic views, towering rows of crags, a hermitage built into a cliff and a challenging steep gully are only a few of the enticing diversions along this circular walk, half of which touches on the more isolated areas of the mountains.

Animal turned to stone: L'Elefant.

From the **Plaça del Monestir**, at first follow Walk 46 (Cim de Sant Jeroni) but at the »Placeta de Santa Anna« continue on the GR trail to the right (markings on the flat rock at the trail's edge). Pass a little viewing point and then at the fork following shortly after, bear left to ascend. Along concrete steps, reach another fork: the white/yellow-marked trail forks left but continue along the GR to the right and pass through a gate. Along the slightly ascending trail, a delightful view opens up to the distant group of crags, known as the »Flautats«. With an unobstructed view of the Pyrenees, the mostly level trail leads to the protruding, flattened slopes of the **Pla de la Trinitat**, 950m, where the white/yellow-marked trail merges again from the left. Turning to the north-west and with the most beautiful view of the vertical cliff faces, the trail drops steadily, crosses a stream bed and then forks shortly afterwards. Now bear left along the white/yellow-marked trail that leads into a gully and crosses another stream bed. Just after, at a cairn (also a white arrow on rock) turn left onto a forest path and immediately begin the ascent in the Canal Plana. Not exactly well-trodden, but easy to discern, the path winds in a constantly steep ascent, at first to the right of the stream bed, then crossing it further up, ascending along the ridge of the Serra de Lluernes and then merging with an intersecting trail. Here, turn left onto the narrow yellow-marked trail thickly overgrown on both sides. In front of a craggy summit, the trail bends left up to a rocky saddle with the Cim de Sant Salvador in view and, after some short stretches through wood, bends directly for the striking »L'Elefant«. In front of the towering crag (a favourite for rock-climbers) and at the undercut base of the rock to the left of the trail, is a delightful place to take a break. At the fork just following, bear left to ascend to the tiny cliff hermitage **Sant Salvador**, 1030m, used by rock-climbers as a *refugi*. Return to the fork, then descend very steeply through forest and meet up with the white/yellow-marked trail; turn right, pass through a gate and then pass by the Sant Benet chapel on the right-hand side of the trail. Along concrete steps and rocky terrain, climb down to the GR and turn right to return to **Plaça del Monestir**.

The cliff face hermitage Sant Salvador.

48 Camino de la Serra Larga

Hubbub and solitude, hand in hand: walking in the south-eastern region of Montserrat

Plaça del Monestir – Capella de la Santa Cova – Pla de Sant Miquel – Plaça del Monestir

Starting point: Plaça del Monestir, 710m. The paying car park in front of the monastery grounds.
Walking times: Plaça del Monestir – Capella de la Santa Cova ½ hr, Capella de la Santa Cova – Pla de Sant Miquel 1 Std; Pla de Sant Miquel – Plaça del Monestir ½ hr; total time 2 hrs.
Ascent: About 150m.
Grade: An easy walk.
Trail markings: Some stretches along the GR-172 (white/red).
Refreshment: None en route; bars and restaurants on the Plaça del Monestir.
Map: Montserrat (Parc Natural), 1:10,000 (Editorial Alpina).

Information: The Oficina de Turisme de Montserrat; ⓒ 93.8777777.
Combination possible: With Walk 46: Cim de Sant Jeroni
Alternative: Extend the walk to **Pla de les Taràntules**, 980m, with a superb view. At the Pla de Sant Miquel, turn left onto the wide track »Camí de les Ermites« and ascend to Pla de les Taràntules; from there, ride down on the »Funicular de Sant Joan«; additional walking time ½ hr (not including the ride down!).
Tip: Walk out the protuding viewing point »Creu de Sant Miquel« along the return route.

A wide and somewhat overblown »way of the Cross« leads to the spectacularly-situated Santa Cova chapel – and here the tourist storm suddenly vanishes: the flower-bedecked lofty mountain path at the foot of the impressive sheer cliffs of the Serra Larga, leading high above the Llobregat Valley, is the exclusive realm of the walker. A serene trail with exquisite views from near and far.

At the car park, follow the road to **Plaça del Monestir**. Near the summit station of the »Funicular de Santa Cova«, take the wide trail signed for »Santa Cova«. This leads past the »Teleféric de Montserrat« and afterwards, along steadily descending steps, crosses the gorge of the »Torrent de Santa María« near the valley station of the »Funicular de Santa Cova«. Continue on to the large cross at the foot of the group of towering crags and, past these, the chapel comes into view,

Along the Camino de la Serra Larga.

clinging to the cliff wall. About 200m before the **Capella de la Santa Cova**, 643m, fork away left onto a trail (wooden sign »Sant Miquel«). This passes below the chapel and in a leisurely ascent traverses the slopes of the Serra Larga; the crag towers reach to the heavens above, while deep down below – the Llobregat Valley. The view to the rear sweeps over the mountains of Sant Llorenç and Montseny all the way to the Pyrenees.

At a signpost, meet up with the GR 172 ascending from Collbató (→ Alternative); turn right here to ascend in the direction »Camí de Sant Miquel«. After a sudden change in direction (northwards) the trail continues in bends, ascending through open slopes to **Pla de Sant Miquel**, 850m and then meets up with a concrete-paved track.

Turning left leads to the Pla de les Taràntules (→ Alternative), a right turn begins the return route along the »Camí de Sant Miquel«. This descends easily, passes the »Sant Miquel« chapel, after which, and to the right, an excursion can be made to the little panoramic viewing point at the »Creu de Sant Miquel«; at the end, through a shady wood, descend to **Plaça del Monestir**.

49 Montgrós, 1118m

Atop the pivoting point of Montserrat

Monestir de Santa Cecília – Coll de Migdia – Montgrós and back

Starting point: The car park at km 5,4 on the BP-1103, 680m, near the Monestir de Santa Cecília. Approaching from Monistrol, drive past the Monestir and about 200m further on, park at the lay-by on the right. Just on the other side of the road, steps begin at the signed trail.
Walking times: Monestir de Santa Cecília – Coll de Migdia 1¼ hrs, Coll de Migdia – Montgrós 1¼ hrs, return 2¼ hrs; total time 4¾ hrs.
Ascent: About 570m.
Grade: Sure-footedness and scrambling

skills are required for the sometimes very steep ascents and descents.
Trail markings: Various coloured markings and directional signs.
Refreshment: None en route; bars and restaurants on the Plaça del Monestir.
Map: Montserrat (Parc Natural), 1:10,000 (Editorial Alpina).
Information: The Oficina de Turisme de Montserrat; ℗ 93.8777777.
Tip: The beautifully-situated Monestir de Santa Cecília with a sensational view of the north face of Montserrat.

A better view of the interior of the Montserrat massif can hardly be had as that from Montgrós. The mountain is set off a little to the south of the main mountain chain and thus presents an unobstructed view of the most beau-

On the Montgrós: surrounded by spectacular rock formations.

tiful crag clusters of Montserrat: from the Agulles to the west over Frares and Ecos, Tabor with the Cim de Sant Jeroni and all the way to Tebaida and Tebes eastwards. Any walker who has only a day to spend in Montserrat would do well to concentrate on Montgrós, even though this mountain is no push-over.

Across the road from the car park near the **Monestir de Santa Cecília**, take the stepped trail of the »Camí de la Font del Llum«. Here are also signs for »Montgròs« and »Ecos«. The white/red-marked trail immediately forks; turn right to continue and ascend until reach-ing yet another junction with signs.

Here, leave the GR behind (this continues to the right to Coll de Can Maçana) by turning left onto the orange-marked trail. After a stretch of strenuous ascent, the trail forks. The path to the right leads in a few min-utes to the »Font del Llum« which is worth seeing; the little spring at the foot of a cliff face is sheltered by a gigantic leaning slab of rock. Back to the trail, ascend along the wooded slopes, always steeply and sometimes strenuously, with a short stretch along a gully, until reaching the **Coll de Migdia**, 1138m. From here, immediately descend steeply again along a white-marked forest path (ignore the blue/yellow marked trail forking right to the »Ecos«). Continuing the descent, reach yet another fork in the trail; ignore the yellow-marked trail forking left and continue to a slight clearing to reach the »Camí de Montgrós«, turning off to the right and marked by wooden signs for »Font Cadireta« and »Montgrós«. Now follow the yellow markings. Immediately begin a strenuous ascent. After a few minutes and near a small, rocky slope, pass by the »Font de la Cadireta« situated a few metres above the trail and then reach the foot of a massive cliff face. Here, a narrow ledge continues the route and leads from time to time as a pas-sageway between the walls of the cliffs.

The trail now splits away from the cliffs, ascends steeply again and reaches an open terrain where it takes a bend to the right. After crossing a little rocky slope, ascend again through forest until reaching a tiny saddle with blue markings. Turn left here and ascend along the bare ridgeline that steadily broadens over the expansive summit of **Montgrós**, 1118m, marked with cairns.

139

50 Agulles Circular Walk

The renowned »pincushion« in the western range of Montserrat

Coll de Can Maçana – Refugi Vicenç Barbé – Coll d'Agulles – Coll de Can Maçana

Starting point: The car park on the Coll de Can Maçana along the BP-1101, 720m.
Walking times: Coll de Can Maçana – Refugi Vicenç Barbé 1 hr, Refugi Vicenç Barbé – Coll d'Agulles ½ hr, Coll d'Agulles – Coll de Can Maçana 1¼ hrs; total time 2¾ hrs.
Ascent: About 320m.
Grade: Sure-footedness and a little scrambling skill is required. The descent from the Coll d'Agulles is quite steep.
Trail markings: Various coloured markings.
Refreshment: Refugi Vicenç Barbé (see Notice); El Bruc.
Map: Montserrat (Parc Natural), 1:10,000 (Editorial Alpina).

Information: The Oficina de Turisme de Montserrat; ✆ 93.8777777.
Notice: There are wardens at the Refugi Vicenç Barbé at the weekend and in the summer. The self-catering hut offers room for 20 people and is mostly used by rock-climbers. A very limited selection of food and drink is available. Information through the FEEC: ✆ 934.120777.
Tip: The picturesque olive groves at the south face of Montserrat and the Can Vinyanova farmstead set before a marvellous backdrop of mountain scenery and offering superb cuisine at the weekend are worth a visit. From El Bruc, drive along the track signed for Can Jorba and Vinyanova.

Capricious but powerful is the impression made by the Agulles (literally: needles) in the western region of Montserrat. The bizarrely eroded rock towers rise up to the heavens out of the dense Mediterranean forest and not only treat walkers to a diverse natural spectacle – rock-climbers too find a veritable paradise here. Those preferring to keep both feet on solid ground are rewarded along this circular walk with an all-encompassing tableau of the Agulles region, including beautiful sweeping views even as far as the Pyrenees.

At the car park on the **Coll de Can Maçana**, take the white/red-marked GR 172 starting at the blocked-off dirt road and at the fork just following, bear left. After the initial ascent, the road levels out – the broad face of the

Agulles appears before; to the left is the Roca Foradada, a triangular rock spur, riddled with holes, and a curious rock formation – la Cadireta – topping it off. The view to the left stretches to the Pyrenees. Along the way, ignore a road forking right and, a little later, reach the Coll de Guirló. Along the extensive saddle, leave the GR and turn right onto the

»Camí de la Portella« (wooden sign »Al Refugi« on a tree). The yellow-marked forest path leads along the foot of the Agulles to a narrow breach in the rock. Starting off with a few scrambling handholds, then along easy, stepped rock, climb up to a small saddle, the »Portella«. Here, the trail forks: to the left and red-marked, the »Travessa de les Agulles« begins, however, descend along the still yellow-marked trail to the right that leads through a lovely wood. Soon the hut comes into view, but just before, the trail forks yet again; bear left (yellow arrow) onto the ascending trail to the **Refugi Vicenç Barbé**, 900m. From the hut, continue along the yellow-marked trail that immediately forks again: to the right and yellow-marked, the trail continues to the Coll de Porc, however, head straight on along the white-marked »Camí de la Canal Ampla«. The trail follows a dry stream bed and ascends almost as straight as an arrow through the broad, wooded

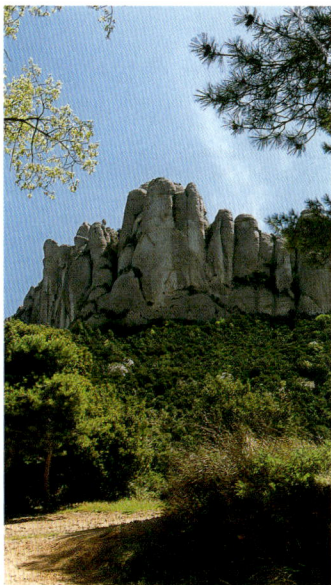

Impressively posed: the famous Agulles.

gully. After a short but strenuous ascent, reach a fork at the foot of a chimney-shaped crag with a faded yellow inscription »Coll d'Agulles«. Bear left following the white markings and after a few minutes reach the **Coll d'Agulles**, 1000m, where the red-marked Agulles cross trail joins up from the left. On the other side of the Coll, climb into the steep, wooded gully that passes between the cliff walls. Along the yellow-marked path, descend in many, and also precipitous, bends. As the steepness of the grade begins to lessen, the trail bends to the right, begins a slight descent and then meets up with a trail ascending from the left. Turn onto this and climb down to the junction of the GR 172; turn left here. The fantastic high mountain trail leads along the foot of the vertically towering crags, skirts around the Roca Foradada, then cuts along the edge of the majestic cliff face of the Agulles, appearing like a row of gigantic organ pipes. Now the trail returns to the Coll de Guirló. From here, take the previously walked route back to the **Coll de Can Maçana**.

Index

alt	altitude	monasteri	monastery
badia	large bay	paratge	landscape
balma	a sheltered habitation built into a cliff wall, cave	parc natural	natural park
		pic	peak, summit
		pla	plain, level area
barranc	mountain stream, gorge	plaça (major)	square, (main square)
can	farmstead	platja	beach
cal	farmstead	pont	bridge
cala	bay, beach inlet	port	port, harbour
camí	trail, route	puig	mountain, summit
cap	cape		
capella	chapel	punta	point, cape
carrer	road	rec	stream, brook
cascada	waterfall	refugi	shelter
castell	castle	riera	stream
cim	peak	riu	river
coll, collet	pass, saddle	roc	crag
cova	cave	santuari	pilgrim's chapel
ermita	hermitage	sender	trail
església	church	serra	mountain range
font	spring	torre	tower
lac, llac	lake	torrent	mountain stream
mas	farmstead		
mirador	viewing point	vall	valley

Abbreviations

GR
Sendero de Gran Recorrido

long-distance trail; red/white markings

PRC
Sendero de Pequeño Recorrido de Catalunya

Catalonian Pyrenees walking trail; white/yellow or only yellow markings

SL
Sender local

local walking trail